How to Build a Million Dollar Database™

There's Power in Who You Know & How Well You Know Them!

gquist

Pink Tomato Publishing

How to Build a Million Dollar Database™
There's Power in Who You Know & How Well You Know Them!

Written by Michelle Bergquist
Layout by CoCo & Associates, Inc.
Published by Pink Tomato Publishing
Copyright 2008 by Michelle Bergquist

Cataloging-in-Publication Data is on file with the Library of Congress
ISBN: 978-0-615-24684-0

PRINTED IN THE UNITED STATES OF AMERICA
First Edition: August, 2008

SPECIAL SALES
Books are available at special discounts for bulk purchases for sales promotions or premiums. Special editions, including personalized covers, excerpts of existing books, and corporate imprints, can be created in large quantities for special needs. For more information, write to Special Sales at Pink Tomato Publishing, specialsales@pinktomatopublishing.com .

To my Mom
For helping me believe I can do whatever I set my mind to!

To my Joe
Love you bunches!

How Important is 'Knowing People' to the Success of What You Do?

Today's Successful Business Pro's Know. . .
It's Not What You Know. . .
It's Not Even Who You Know. . .
It's What You Do With Who You Know!

This book is dedicated to all the business professionals committed to building priceless business relationships. Enjoy!!

- Michelle Bergquist

Business Consultant, Author, Trainer & Speaker

How to Build a Million Dollar Database™ - There's Power in Who You Know and How Well You Know Them!

Contents

Introduction

"Relationships Make The World Work"

What I Believe
I believe that relationships are the key to business success.
For over 25 years I've experienced first hand how important
relationships can be to business introductions, new business
opportunities, career connections, promotions, transfers,
referrals and business favors and contacts just by who
you know and how well you know them. Relationships
are how business gets done and how people get access to
opportunities and connections.

A Philosophy Of Building Relationships
It takes a different mindset to realize how powerful
relationships can be to business and success. When you
realize the more you know someone and how beneficial
that can be to working smarter as opposed to harder in
business, why would you choose to work any other way?
I've found so many opportunities in business and in life
by the relationships I've built with my clients, colleagues,
former business partners, former bosses and co-workers.

I've kept in touch with many, lost touch with a few and
reconnected with yet a few more. Along the way, I've found

how valuable my business relationships have been when I first gave, and then received. I firmly believe that things get done by who you know and how well you know them.

I don't mean to convey that building relationships is about "using people." You've gotta' give before you get. Successful professionals have an attitude of gratitude and the mindset that when you give you get. This book offers a system in how to keep connected with your important business relationships. In addition, this book outlines a strategy of coding your key relationships so you can organize who you stay connected to, how often, and how to track what you know about them. This book also offers a solution to organizing your contacts so you don't have to rely on your brain to remember key relationship information.

What I Know For Sure
In the hundreds and hundreds of interviews from clients and attendees over the years I can tell you that 99% of professionals in business want to do a better job in building relationships. Relationships are the central key to being more successful in business. Everyone wants to have a better connection with the people they do business with or rely on for opportunities and connections. The challenge is how to develop a systematic process to stay in touch to build better relationships.

The Walking Rolodex
In the early 90's, one of my business partners called me the "The Walking Rolodex" and it caught on with other contacts and referral partners. I never realized at that time what a compliment it was, as I always loved being a resource to the people I met through networking, along with those I did

business with and referred business to. When they needed to get information on someone or find a service or product provider, I was the "go-to" person for information and referrals. I loved being a connector and a resource. While I used to laugh when called "The Walking Rolodex," I now realize how important a good system is to keep track of contacts and relationships.

I finally realized the importance of relationships to success when I started using some of the connections I had developed from all the years of giving and providing value and opportunity. In my transition from one career and business to the next, and from one location to another, I was able to tap into the resources I had developed over the years. It was then that I saw how important priceless relationships are to business and success. My business contacts and relationships provided me with referrals, contacts, connections, letters of testimonial and personal introductions I never could have made if I hadn't had such strong relationships with the people I knew.

The Million Dollar Database™
In the early days of being a business professional, I started to keep my contacts in a database that I kept up-to-date and in one central place where I housed my contacts and relationships. Back in the day I only kept contact information on my business and personal contacts and this book is the culmination of what I've learned in segmenting, rating, sorting and tracking information about all my key relationships. I used the database in the beginning as a list to house contacts so I didn't have to rely on my brain or pieces of paper to remember information.

In later years, I started to use my database as the one central tool in keeping more detailed information about my contacts than a name, address and phone number. I started to keep track of people's birthdays and note special information about them and their family and business information so I could quickly access information and data.

What I learned from keeping a database all these years is how easily you can communicate with all your contacts and relationships if you just keep your list up-to-date and organized. What I also learned is how difficult it is to maintain and keep your database up-to-date.

Selfishly, I also learned how valuable keeping your own contact list is if you work for someone else. I experienced 5 mergers and acquisitions during my banking career and was always thankful that I kept my customer information and contacts on index cards (this was before personal computers). When the mergers and acquisitions happened, nobody had time to re-create their contact lists and I learned early on not to rely on the company approved customer data files, as I never knew when I would be in transition, yet again.

In the late 90's I formed a corporate gift company called The Corporate Basket and again I utilized my database to contact all my key relationships to let them know of the new business venture I was involved in. I learned how valuable former colleagues, business associates, bosses and co-workers are when you transition from one career or business opportunity to the next. It's the single most important lesson I've learned in life and business. You may know thousands of people, but if you don't maintain communication with those you know and who you knew from the past, you will miss opportunity and connections because you've lost touch.

Who This Book is Dedicated To

This book is for the professionals in business and the business development pro's who want a more effective way to connect and relate to the business people they know and have relationships with. This book is about a better way to build relationships and do better business!

Most business books tell you to keep a database of your contacts and connections. They never spell out the process and manner in which to communicate and relate to your contacts and connections. This book does just that. I've taken sales training and sales development programs only to be left searching for a viable system to keep track of my contacts, business partners, prospects, referral partners and customers. I've learned powerful processes in how to sell, but no system of follow-up, communicating and relating with my relationships and important contacts. In the 25 years I've been in business, this is the system I've developed that has worked for me in developing millions and millions of dollars worth of opportunity and connections.

The system outlined in this book doesn't happen overnight. It takes time and patience to build a Million Dollar Database™. This book isn't a "techie" book on how to build a Million Dollar Database™. At the heart of my message is a system and method to connect with your important business relationships, along with suggestions on how to communicate with those you want to build better relationships with.

We live in a hi-tech, impersonal and electronic world, where the personal touch is more critical than ever in developing a communication system that helps you build and maintain long lasting, powerful business relationships. I hope you'll enjoy this book and look to make changes in how you communicate and relate to the business relationships you hold critical to success for you and your business!

The
Foundation

"If you can't do great things, do small things in a great way. Don't wait for great opportunities. Seize common, everyday ones and make them great." - Napoleon Hill

Foundation and Benefits

At the cornerstone of a Million Dollar Database™ is a philosophy that it's not what you know in business or even who you know, but what you do with who you know! You may be the best professional networker in your business community and have a large database of contacts that total thousands, but if you hold your contacts in an electronic database and do nothing with them, you've got nothing of value except names and numbers. I strongly encourage you to apply the techniques suggested throughout this book. If you're the busy professional who's never had time to enter your contacts into a database, you'll benefit by reconnecting with lost customers, contacts and referral sources and maintain ongoing communication with your important business relationships.

Ask yourself how much more successful you could be if you went deeper in knowledge and information about your important relationships and contacts? How much more successful could you be if you took a different approach in communication to actually know your relationships so well that you could actually 'wow" them and stay top of mind to only think of you as the person who does what you do!?

If you're looking for more new customers, repeat business from your existing customers, improved loyalty from your existing client base and more referrals and introductions to new business, these are the benefits that await you in reading and implementing How to Build a Million Dollar Database™!

It's Not What You Know . . . It's Who You Know . . . Or Is It?!

"Keep Connected. . . .Build Relationships. . . .Achieve Results"

Knowing People is Important to Business Success

There's a saying in business that goes like this: "It's Not What you Know in Business – It's Who You Know" that's important. Never before is that statement more important in business today. Knowing people can be the difference between success and failure. If you're in business for yourself, "who" you know can be the difference between landing an important account or losing a deal to someone because they had a personal introduction to the prospect. If you're a salesperson, "who" you know can make the difference between cold calling day in and day out or landing a big project because you received a personal introduction based on who you know. More than ever before, knowing people is critical to business success.

Let's go one step further. It's not who you know in business, it's how well you know them. Knowing people isn't what determines success in business. There are plenty of successful business professionals who know lots of people. In today's highly competitive business environment, it's not enough to have a database or rolodex full of contacts with names, addresses and phone numbers. In addition, there are plenty of business professionals today who think that collecting email addresses and sending a constant series of e-marketing messages is the best way to build their business. Ask yourself how well you know people and how well do you keep connected with your important business relationships.

This book is about a process designed to help you in organizing the people you know in business and how to develop a communication strategy with those oh-so important relationships so you do better business!

Your Important Business Relationships

The first step to think through in building a Million Dollar Database™ is to evaluate who your most important business relationships are. Most professionals will agree that customers and client relationships are likely the most important category of relationships.

Who else do you define as an important business relationship? Potential customers? Referral sources? Vendors? Categorizing your relationships is one step to better business as you must define the relationship and then work on a method to building a better relationship through communication and interaction. I see many business professionals dump all their relationships, including customers, prospects and referral sources into an email marketing system and then send out blast communications with the same message. Business success today is about creating a custom, personalized communication and follow-up system.

Ask yourself how you categorize your important business relationships. Where did you meet your contacts? More importantly, how do you keep connected and in communication with your important business relationships? Do you keep a list or database of your contacts? Are your contacts located in a place where you can easily access information about your important relationships or are they strewn about in different contact management systems, lists, folders, Post-it® notes and scraps of paper? I've seen more than a few business professionals who continue to keep their important contacts on their desks with notes written on business cards and little rubber bands around them. What kind of information do you keep on your contacts and where do you keep track of your important relationships?

In this book, I'm going to share the details of how to keep information on your relationships to help you in your quest to know people beyond a name, address and email. Knowing people beyond basic contact information can be the subtle difference between making it and making it big in business by building priceless relationships.

It's not enough in this day and age to just "know people." How well do you know your important business relationships? Who you know in business today isn't nearly as important as how well you know them. This book is going to provide you a system in how to know people beyond a name, address and email and how this process of getting to know people can be quite useful to success in business.

Who You Know

Take a look at who you currently know in business. Do you know enough of the right people? I see professionals regularly who talk about their contacts and say they have lots of people in their database but they're filled with the wrong type of individual or company in who they need to know. Are you meeting the right kind of people as you network and build your database? If you're networking, are you missing opportunity because you're evaluating who you meet based on whether they are a potential customer for you, as opposed to delving into who they know and how they might introduce you to opportunity? Have you purchased a cold mailing list or email list in the past and it's not working for you in bringing in business? Are you exhibiting at places that have virtually no chance of landing you leads to follow-up on because the attendees aren't the right fit for you and your business? Take a critical look at who you currently know and ask yourself the following:

- Do you know specifically who you're going after to gain business and opportunity?
- Do you have enough people in your database of the specific-type professionals and/or people who can refer you business?
- Do you have enough people in your database who are in front of the people you'd like to do business with and be introduced to?
- Do you have enough people in your database that know you and what you're looking for in the way of business?

- Do you have enough people in your database who see you as a go-to resource for the people you currently do business with?
- Do you have referral partners and professionals listed in your database so you can refer to them when the opportunity comes about?
- Do you know specifically who your best customers are and do you know them well enough through staying connected and in touch for repeat business and opportunity?
- Do you have enough prospects listed in your database to convert those prospects into paying customers?
- Do you consistently add new contacts and meet new people to add to your contact list for opportunity and connections?

If you answered "no" to any of the above questions, this book will help you in your goal to do better business and build more effective relationships!

Evaluating Who You Know

Evaluating who you know is a starting point for improvement to building better relationships. Start today by taking a concerted effort to get all your contacts into one database system and/or contact management system. One key to success in business is realizing that you need to know people well in order to "woo" business, develop repeat business and ask for referrals. If you find that you're cold calling all the time, are you putting those contacts into your database or contact management system to start the process of building a relationship with those individuals? Do you follow-up with those you've gotten business cards from? Do you only call people to give them your pitch for products or services? Later in this book, I'll be laying out strategies in how to build rapport and better business relationships. For now, ask yourself if you're the "hit-and-run" type of sales professional? Hit 'em with your pitch and then move on and never contact them again because they said "not now" in your first pitch? Sales training programs I've been involved with talk about how to make your pitch and move on from one prospect to the next. In the system I'll be explaining throughout this book, you'll see that prospects who don't buy today might be worth thousands and in some cases millions based on timing and continued communication and interaction.

The more you realize that it takes time to get to know people and build relationships, the better you'll see how important having a Million Dollar Database™ is to success. The database tool allows you the opportunity to use technology as a way to interact with your contacts and maintain top of mind awareness through your communication, message and interaction. The same thing applies when you meet someone new. People don't refer business immediately to someone they just met, as well as people don't typically do business with someone they have just been introduced to. It takes time and nurturing to build relationships and your job in evaluating who you know is to realize that you've got to have a system in place to get to know people or you're just playing the numbers in landing new accounts and new business. This is the old way of doing business and it's not effective anymore!

From today on, tell yourself that your job is to have the mindset that anyone you meet might have potential for you down the road and your job is to begin the process in building a relationship with those you meet. Through interaction and communication, you'll determine the potential value of that relationship and through your database you can flag the individual as to what value they bring or might bring to you and your business. You never know how the people you meet might be a resource for you in the future.

Career Connections from Knowing People

Time has been spent evaluating how contacts can be used to bring in new business for sales development, but much of what I'm talking about can be applied for better career connections, job transitions and promotions. What would you do tomorrow if you got laid off and your employer shut off all access to your database and office contacts?

Over and over I've seen professionals who have put all their contacts on the company database and have their contacts in the company approved contact management system that are surprised and frustrated when they're laid off or down sized and they now have no access to their contacts or business relationships. These contacts are now considered "work product" and inaccessible now that you've been laid off or denied access to your office resources. Keep your own set of contacts and relationships in a separate contact management system apart from the company database and system.

When you're in transition, down-sized or laid off, the last thing you want to do is pull together your old contacts and try to find them again, or worse, try to get access to them from a former employer. In this day and age with technology and computers, you should be using your own database as a professional and be at the ready to zip out communication with former colleagues, contacts, vendors, suppliers and relationships. Keep track of the associations you previously belonged to, along with the members of those associations and your former vendor and supplier relationships, as these folks can be tremendous resources for you in job transition or future career connections.

You never know when you're going to be in a position that "who you know" comes into play with job promotions and career connections, so maintain your own database of contacts and build communication on your own to keep connected, outside of the company sponsored communication. This may prove to be critical in the future for your career and job growth and transition.

The People Connection

A major part of success in business is to review how you relate to people and connect person-to-person. With our reliance today on technology for efficiency and productivity, we've lost the personal touch that's a major piece to business success. People do business and refer business to people they know, they like, they trust and respect. What kind of job are you doing building a personal connection with the people you meet and that you do business with? If you're not getting enough referrals, ask yourself what kind of job you're doing in maintaining a relationship with those who have referred you business in the past? Do you connect with them beyond the cursory email message that's blasted out to everyone in your database on a regular basis? What about those who have referred business to you more than once? How often do you engage with them as a top notch referral source and show your appreciation so they keep sending you more business? How much repeat business are you getting from your existing customers and client relationships? Are you relying on the company you work for to send out the obligatory seasonal holiday cards that are sent to everyone on the client list? Now's the time to evaluate how you connect with your important business relationships one-to-one and review how you relate to the people you know.

The person-to-person connection means that you need to move beyond technology and get to the "personal" side of people relations. I'm not talking about "fru-fru" business relations, but a relationship that takes into account getting to know someone beyond the business transaction and name, address and email. How often do you call and/or personally email your key relationships? When's the last time you actually spoke with one of your key contacts via phone or in person? Most professionals I talk to and that I've researched tell me they try to maintain the personal connection, but it's overwhelming today in keeping track of the person-to-person connections, so they just don't do it or don't have a system in how to keep on top of who's been contacted and when they've been contacted.

Building a Million Dollar Database™ is about using technology in a way to keep track of who you've talked to and when, so you work smarter, not harder in maintaining business relationships. As you go through this book, I'll show you a number of key tools, strategies and follow-up methods to track and monitor who you've recently called and/or communicated with. You'll be more organized in your interaction and follow-up, which will help you be more effective in building priceless relationships!

Important and Influential Contacts

Keeping track of who you know in business can lead to incredible opportunities. I've found that tracking key influencers within certain industries and having a relationship with key contacts in that industry lead to opportunities I never thought of and introductions that I was blessed to receive because of my relationship with others. Knowing people is central to success. Knowing people well can lead to additional opportunities and introductions that you've never dreamed of.

Somebody Versus Anybody

It's important to note that you need to be clear about what you're trying to accomplish and who you want to meet through introductions and connections. A client of mine, Paul, who sold commercial insurance, was looking to make connections into the biotech industry in San Diego, California. He had lots of connections within the legal and financial services industry, but wanted to make in-roads into the biotech and pharmaceutical industry locally.

Instead of cold calling and telemarketing like many insurance professionals are taught to do, my client began to attend the local BIOCOM industry association meetings for those in the industry to connect and gather. Paul didn't meet a lot of decision makers at these breakfast meetings, however, he did meet those who served the biotech industry and learned quickly through conversation and research who the key companies were in San Diego and who the decision makers were that he should be in front of. Instead of telemarketing to make appointments with these professionals, Paul worked back with other key supplier relationships and contacts he had as business and referral partners to see if anyone knew any of these professionals directly that he wanted to be introduced to. He met with his legal partners that served the biotech industry and asked each contact if anyone knew or had a connection to the person he was looking to meet. In his database, he noted each contact that could be a person of influence and he communicated very clearly who it was he was looking for an introduction to. Paul began to get introductions to the people he was looking for. Slowly, strategically, Paul began to acquire introductions and get known within this industry as a professional who could provide value added services to the biotech industry. This process didn't happen overnight, but if Paul hadn't been clear about who he wanted to know and who he was looking to be introduced to, he never would have made the connections as quickly as he had.

He noted the persons of influence in his database and coded who knew and referred him to each contact and then began a follow-up and communication system that I'll talk about later in this book to build a relationship with top industry influencers. This is one of many success stories in how to use your Million Dollar Database™ as a successful method to meet industry leaders and influencers. It's all in how you go about the process and how you follow-up and communicate to make connections.

Do You Know Enough Of The Right People?

Ask yourself if you know enough of the right people to be successful in your line of work. I work with professionals all the time who tell me how many contacts they have in their database, like it's a badge of glory to have obtained thousands of contacts in their system. This is the last thing I'm trying to convey in how to build a Million Dollar Database™. Relationships are central to business success. Quality in the number of people and the depth of the relationship is the foundation to finding opportunity, new business and referrals.

The big question remains, do you know enough of the right people for opportunity in leads, new business, referrals and sales? In other words, are you targeted in your efforts to meet the right people and go deep within the community or industry? I always suggest to clients that you take a look at your key client relationships and referral relationships and ask yourself if you're known within the industry and/or community you serve? If you find that you only know a few key companies or individuals, then your job is to get known within a specific target industry or community. Get known within an industry association or community group so that you build relationships with people that might be able to open doors of opportunity for you or lead you to other key contacts and professionals you'd like to know. This is a process that doesn't happen overnight and takes quite a bit of strategy and patience in execution. In future chapters, I'll explain the process of how to get to know contacts beyond just association in an organization or group. For now, make plans to start entering every contact you meet in the community or association into your database.

People You Would Like To Know

Another strategy to building a Million Dollar Database™ is to think and keep track of those individuals or key persons of influence you'd like to know or get an introduction to. When you read or hear about or learn of key professionals that you'd like to know in the future, use your database as a place to note the contact and make a concerted effort to plant seeds with those who might provide an introduction and/or referral to in the future. One of my favorite phrases is, "If you don't ask, you don't get." You've got to be specific in who you'd like to know in order to receive introductions and/or referrals to. Your Million Dollar Database™ is a key place to flag these future contacts as people you'd like to know and find those who might provide an introduction. Your database is also a place to start a communication plan with or find others who might provide a warm introduction for opportunity. The key thing is you've got to ask and you've got to be clear about who you want to know. Keep track of the individuals in your database and log information you learn about them so you start to build a relationship and get to know people over time.

This system works whether you're looking to bring in a new client or if you're a career professional and you're looking to gain ground in a new industry or make a change within the industry you currently work in. It's no longer effective to find the best jobs through online ads or through the human resources departments of organizations. The way to find the best positions for career growth are the ones you find by gaining access to other hiring managers and decision makers within companies and industries. How do you meet these people? The more contacts you have within the industry you'd like to be working in, the more you can find introductions into the new industry you're looking to be accepted into.

A colleague of mine used their database as a way to find new industry leaders. Dave put contacts into his database and flagged persons of influence in the industry he was trying to gain access into with a career change. Dave spent time researching the local industry leaders and began a series of personalized communications to each of the industry leaders on a frequent basis. He sent a letter of inquiry and notes asking for an informational meeting. He landed quite a few informational interviews that gave him access to professionals he'd never met before. As he met each individual, he would ask for insight into the industry, things to keep in mind, and ask if there was anyone else he should talk to. After about 10 or so informational interviews, Dave received an introduction to a VP of Finance that was looking for someone new to bring into his department at a senior level. My colleague Dave not only landed a sweet job in a different industry, he was able to get the interview and land the job before the position even posted in the online community. Wow! There's an example of the power of making new connections on those people you'd like to know better!

Keeping Track Of Relationships

Number one on the hardship list of professionals is how to keep track of relationships and organize key contacts into a system that keeps you up-to-date and on top of who you know and when you've contacted them. The first challenge for any professional is getting your contacts loaded into a contact management system or database system. The second challenge is to organize those relationships to begin the process of staying connected and in communication with them to find opportunity, new business and referrals.

Start today and realize that you must either enter in contacts yourself or pay someone to enter contacts into your database and keep your contacts organized and up-to-date. If you're a small business owner, look at database management just like you do your accounting process. It's not the fun part of running a business, but it's critical to being a success in what you do. If you're a sales professional, realize that this is how you can work smarter, not harder, in bringing in the right kind of business and landing more sales. The key message here is, if you won't keep your database up-to-date, pay someone to help you keep it up-to-date.

2

Building Priceless Relationships - The Big Payoff to Business Success

"Things we do for people are usually among the best things we do." - CD Jackson

Hit 'Em and Run Doesn't Work Anymore

We live in a "fast food world." Immediate gratification is what we look for in wealth, success and opportunity. What's wrong with this mind-set is that building relationships to land new customers, repeat business and referrals takes time, strategy and patience. This is how successful businesses work today. More organizations should teach this in their sales training and sales development courses. The "hit 'em and run" philosophy of business doesn't work anymore. People have too many options and choices in who they do business with. The pitch 'em and run philosophy taught by many sales development programs don't work anymore. They're ineffective. Successful professionals today know that building priceless relationships take time but they have a big payoff in the end. Your job is to build a relationship with others so they make the decision to buy themselves.

You lead them to water by showing them you're the best option of alternative solutions. This takes time.

Today's statistics and reports show at least seven or more touches of interaction and communication are needed to "woo" someone to do business with you or refer business to you. Change your mindset and change your results. Focus today on building enough opportunity in your pipeline so you're landing new customers and following up on referrals like never before. When people know you, like you and trust you they're more likely to do business with you.

Start today and realize the people you meet or those given a proposal have a high probability of not buying from you right away. Your job as a sales professional is to "woo" them into doing business with you over time. People do business with people they know, they like, they trust and respect. This process can't be rushed.

The Power of Following Up and Staying in Touch

Jenny, a professional in the placement industry, was looking to "woo" a distribution company over to using their placement and temporary staffing services. Jenny had done all the right things to uncover opportunity and submit a proposal to the distribution company, however, the company continued to use their existing staffing company for services.

Jenny didn't give up. She followed up. She sent information about what to look for in selecting the right staffing company. She sent seasonal cards just to stay in touch and maintain communication with the head of human resources at the distribution company. Jenny even went so far as to fire off an email frequently just to stay connected and see if there was an opportunity for her and her company to be of service. She kept asking each time she spoke with the human resources contact for the opportunity to be of service. Jenny kept notes in her database and noted the conversations, dates and comments from each touch point of communication. After about five months of calling, sending and communicating Jenny received her first job order from the Human Resources Director of the distribution company. They were unhappy with their current provider and wanted to see what Jenny and her company would do in providing a temporary staff person for eight weeks while one of their key account service clerks was on maternity leave. That first job order led to a few others and by the end of the year Jenny had a contract for all of the distribution company's staffing service needs. The lesson: timing and follow-up works!

Here's the big lesson. Jenny didn't give up on the follow-up. She kept in touch and made a point to check in with the Human Resources Director at the distribution company. Jenny made sure to never lose touch and collected little bits and pieces of information about the Human Resources Director through their interaction in person and over the phone. She invited her to lunch on the anniversary of using their staffing services and learned what her company had done right, what should be improved or changed. In addition, Jenny learned a lot of other intelligence through her communication and interaction with her client. She logged all this in her database so as to note special and key personal information about her client. On her client's birthday, she sent a bouquet of flowers. Not just any flowers, but her client's favorite colored roses. Is it any wonder that this distribution company has been a loyal, dedicated client to Jenny for almost six years? What do you do before, during and after the sale to maintain a strong connection and relationship with your key customers?

The Time Factor to Building Relationships

Timing is a key factor to building priceless relationships and landing new business. You may be in a situation where you have a potential client who's interested in doing business with you but, for whatever reason, they are staying with the same service provider they currently have. I have many long-term clients that I've landed new business with, not because I gave them a slick proposal or probed them into closing scenarios that prompted them to buy. I was able to "woo" them over as a new customer because I took the time to get to know them and was patient knowing that "timing" has a significant aspect to gaining new business. I sent them information frequently and checked in personally over a period of time to see if we could step up and be of service. At the time many of my clients got fed-up with their existing service provider, we were top of mind in getting them to use our services. Realize that a significant amount of business is left on the table because professionals forget to follow-up and have no system to maintain communication with potential customers. In future chapters, I'll show you many examples of communication methods to use your database to land business as a result of being in the right place at the right time and creating top of mind awareness.

The Follow-up Factor

Historically, statistic after statistic shows that almost 40% of business is left on the table because professionals don't follow-up and stay in communication to land new business. Whether it's new accounts or repeat business from existing customer relationships, timing and follow-up have a significant impact on your success in business.

Your database and how you use it can be the central key to success which allows you to be 40% more effective in gaining new business, repeat business and referrals. Keep your prospects in your database and develop follow-up communication that allows you to keep connected beyond the "buy-from-me" marketing materials that you constantly send out. Look for small, frequent interactions through face-to-face communication, through the mail, through personalized email and through telephone interactions to stay in touch. Be different than all the others who do what you do and use your database as the core system to following up and landing 40% more business just by staying in touch. In future chapters, I'll show you examples and methods of follow-up that keep you connected with your important business relationships.

The Identity Factor

People reveal their true identity over time and I'm amazed at how often this fact is forgotten in maintaining and building relationships in business. Surface versus depth of the relationship is an important factor to remember. If you truly want to get to know your important business relationships, then time is central to understanding someone and who they really are. We all put on a "professional face" and demeanor and only through time and trust do you get to know the real self of an individual.

Getting to know someone beyond an account number can be critical to gaining referrals from existing customers, and reaping the benefits of additional business with customers you know really well. Take the time to invite your key customers to lunch or dine with them. If you can't dine with clients, as some business relationships don't allow you to give anything of value in gifts or appreciation, focus on a "client annual review" where you sit down with a client and go over the year and how things went, what went well and what can be improved for the future in your business relationship. I've found this a wonderful tool in gleaning information to know a client more than name, address, phone and customer number. Through interactive questions, you can get at the heart of who someone is and get to know them over time and who they really are. This kind of relationship leads to loyalty and the added benefit of referrals and repeat business.

The Profile Factor

Just because you get to know someone beyond name, address and account number doesn't guarantee that this can bring value to you and your business. Profiling and collecting information provides opportunity to communicate and interact with your key relationships in a personal manner. This builds better relationships. This helps you do better business.

The question becomes how to keep track of information you glean through your relationships. What information do you keep track of on your customers and referral relationships and how does that benefit you and your business relationships? Where do you keep track of information you learn about your customers and key relationships? The answer is your database, of course!

A problem I see over and over is what to do when you want to send out information like birthday cards or send gifts to your most valuable and loyal customers. The problem becomes how to keep track and implement the program. If you don't have a system in tracking information and profiling your customers and relationships, you have to rely on your brain or pieces of paper to gather and track information. Today, that kind of system is extremely ineffective. I have many clients who originally had difficulty in sending out holiday cards to their contacts or difficulty in keeping track of personal information and business information on their best business relationships.

With the flexibility of segmenting data and keeping information on relationships in a database system, this allows you the easy option to zip out communication to your relationships quickly and efficiently. In addition, with easy sorting and tracking of information within your database, you can keep information on your customers and relationships without relying on your brain. Just imagine how nice it would be to easily send out gifts of appreciation or zip out communication that's personalized and custom to the individual relationship.

Does your database have a section that allows you to track key preferences and personal information or business information about your key relationships? If it doesn't, you're missing the boat in creating moments of opportunity to build priceless relationships that allow you to generate repeat business and more referrals. In future sections of this book, I'll show you key pieces of information to track and gather on your key relationships that allow you to set yourself apart and build priceless relationships that lead to new business, repeat business and more referrals than ever before!

Know – Like – Trust Factor

Why do you think people buy from you today? Is it because you were the lowest price that bid on the project among you and your competitors? Were you the lowest in price among the choices your customer had in selecting you versus the others who do what you do? More than likely, your customers selected you and your business because they got to know you, they liked you and they trusted you before they chose to do business with you.

The phrase, "know you, like you and trust you" is almost cliché today, but it's so powerful in the reason people decide to do business with you versus the other choices they have. If you find that you're competing on price in your business and losing accounts because people feel that you're too expensive or they can't afford to buy your products or services, then you're not doing justice in building relationships that can take away the problem of affordability, budget or price.

The commodity-driven business process is a thing of the past. People today have so many options in whom they choose to do business with. The goal of every professional today is to find the group of prospects who are concerned with value of the service provider, along with the products and services they sell. What this means to you and your business is that your database is a tool that allows you to research and track the right mix of business and opportunity by finding trends and profiling your customers. This allows you to meet their needs in value and opportunity, beyond the price of your products and services. Later in this book, I'll show you a number of methods to create value and virtually cut out the price issue in landing new business and repeat business.

Brand "U"

*"When Your Words and Actions Match,
People Know They Can Trust You."*

What Do You Want to Be Known For?

If I asked you the question, what do you want to be known for, how would you answer that? Do you want to be known as someone of trust, someone who can be counted on, someone who is honest or goes the extra mile in creating value for your clients and important relationships? I believe those of us in business who are professionals have every good intention of doing what we say we will, but things fall short in execution.

This is an important point in developing business and creating value among the people you'd like to receive referrals from and those you look to for opportunity. So many business professionals over-promise and under-deliver today. Your personal brand, or what I call "Brand U," is something that you need to be aware of and decide on as to what kind of reputation and image you project. Among the people you'd like to do business with and those you look to develop referral opportunities from, what brand are you known for or do you wish you'd be known for?

I can think of many, many instances where business colleagues or sales people have made commitments to send me things that never happen, or people who say they will call and never do. Even professionals who say they will follow-up in a few weeks and have every good intention, but never do. Can you think of all the commitments you've made but, alas, fall short in execution? These actions, whether they're followed through on or not, brand you as a professional.

Commitments aren't the only way to "Brand U." I can think of times in business where I worked on projects with someone who was habitually late to meetings, appointments and out of office events. It seems as though every time I had to meet this person at a dedicated time I could count on the fact they would be late. Their brand came across loud and clear – if you were meeting with this person, it became a joke that you'd better tell them to arrive one half hour earlier so they would be on time. The sad part is, as much I knew this person and how they had no purposeful intention of being late, they were developing a brand as someone you couldn't count on to be on time. They were gaining a reputation and brand as someone who couldn't be counted on. Trust me when I tell you the "brand" you exhibit, good or bad, is hard to change once you get a reputation for exhibiting that kind of behavior. I also need to tell you (confession time) that this wasn't someone I worked with, this was actually me for a long period of time in business and one of the hardest things I've had to work on and overcome!

Your Brand "U"

Begin today in evaluating and changing the "Brand U" that you exhibit for the better. I find that most professionals create their own problems in "Brand U" by over promising and not following through. Start to recognize how you come across through the things you say in commitments and promises. People take you at your word, so what do you say and promise?

Ask yourself what "Brand U" are you exhibiting? If you say you'll do something, or promise something or say you'll follow-up, do you? In our business world today, think through all the things you promise or commit to that go unfulfilled or left undone. With our overworked business society that revolves around a 24/7 world, what you promise and what you say you'll do comes across loud and clear to the people you want to get business from and those you'd like to receive referrals from. Realize that part of our success or failure in business has to do with the reputation and brand we've created for ourselves in business. Start today by taking ownership of your personal "Brand U" and realize that all your actions, both filled or unfulfilled, create a reputation with those who might do business with you and refer business to you.

Part of improving your "Brand U" is to use your database as a tool in flagging follow-up and reminders through your notes and calendar section on items to do or send. This isn't an easy step. Part of the success in building a Million Dollar Database™ is to recognize the areas that need improvement and take steps through systemizing and automating processes so things don't fall through the cracks. Your database should allow you to make notes and set calendar follow-up on commitments so you don't create a negative "Brand U."

Make a point to evaluate how you think you come across to your key contacts and relationships. If you aren't sure how your brand is coming across, have a conversation with one of your trusted advisors, business partners or clients. Ask them what you can do to improve who you are and how you come across. Trust me, it's a tough conversation to have, but one that might provide valuable information and insight. Sometimes the right thing to say is the hardest thing to say. Success starts with how you come across and the reputation you've built, either positive or negative. Work on improving your Brand "U."

Hub Central

"Your Key Relationships Deserve Your Consistent Attention"

Your Database HQ

Central to building a Million Dollar Database™ is to decide where you house your current contacts and relationships. How do you keep track of who you know? Do you have a contact management system or database program to house your contacts and business relationships? Do you have the old fashioned rolodex at your desk where you flip and file to find a contact or business relationship? Are you the individual who has loads and loads of business cards with rubber bands around them just waiting for the right time to get them organized and entered into a system somewhere at sometime down the road? Or, are you waiting for a future date to get your act together and get your contacts into a system beyond the paper directories, spreadsheets and files?

Your first step in building a Million Dollar Database™ is to get your contacts and connections entered into one electronic database system. The database allows you the option to communicate quickly and efficiently while maintaining communication with the contacts you'd like to stay in touch with regularly.

No longer can you rely on the old fashioned folders, pieces of paper and manual systems to build business relationships today. It's not efficient and you can't rely on your brain to remember important dates and items any longer that allow you to stay connected and top of mind. The database, used properly, is the number one way to build better relationships with your key contacts.

The problem most professionals run into is that the one tool that allows you to be more efficient is the one thing that becomes a pain to organize, manage and use to your advantage. The key to success is how you organize, segment, collect intelligence and then communicate to stay top of mind. In later chapters I'll go into detail about ways to stay in touch and keep track of who you know so you come across as a true master relationship builder!

One Central Database

The primary reason to keep your contacts and relationships in one central database is that technology and database management allow you to manipulate, sort and segment your contacts and relationships. This sorting and segmenting allows you to communicate and interact more strategically. With the ability to personalize communication, it doesn't make sense today to send out an email in mass if you don't personalize it. Worse yet, if you send out any form of printed materials and don't personalize the communication, you're missing the boat in gaining a competitive edge for market share and top of mind awareness. With the option to use variable data printing, which allows you to personalize your printed communication, your database allows you to quickly and efficiently zip out a list to your printer who then can personalize and customize your communications. Database technology and tools allow you the flexibility to customize and personalize, while relying on technology to propel you to efficiency and immediacy in communication.

The Connected Yet Disconnected World

While we may live in a technological and digital world, we've become more and more disconnected to the personal approach in building relationships in business. While we need to use technology to make ourselves more efficient and productive, it shouldn't replace the human, personal touch in staying connected.

Think of this book as the process of how to use technology in such a way as to relate in a more relationship-centered way to generate business, repeat business and referrals.

In our electronic and technological world, the personal touch is the best way in cementing long lasting, priceless relationships. Your database is the tool that allows you to use technology as an efficient way to reach out at a personal level and communicate with those you'd like to stay connected to.

The challenge for most business professionals is how to use the technology and set up a series of systems and processes to relate personally. Your database allows you the use of technology to be more efficient and communicate one-to-one. Later in this book I'll talk about how to use your database and the power of segmenting and sorting information as the number one tool to create personal, customized communication. In addition, I'll walk through how to keep track of information and use intelligence you gather so you look like a master to those you do business with and network with.

Selecting Your Database

Choosing a database system becomes a little confusing today, as there are many choices to select from. Later I'll talk more about the systems and action steps to building your Million Dollar Database™. I personally have used the Act! contact management system for almost 15 years since it first came out originally as a desktop solution for contact management (yes, I'm dating myself here). The more popular database and contact management systems today are: Act!, GoldMine®, Salesforce.com, Outlook with Business Contact Manager and Microsoft CRM 4.0. All systems have pros and cons associated with their ease of use, training, costs and application. The system you choose needs to allow you to do the following:

- Ability to enter basic contact information and track and sort via name, address, phone, city, state and email.
- Ability to enter and sort by the title and function of your key contacts and relationships.
- Ability to categorize your contacts according to specific types (client, prospect, referral source, distributor, contact, supplier, key relationships, connections of influence, etc.).
- Ability to segment your contacts and give your relationships a hierarchy of their importance to you and your business (best clients, hot prospects, most

important referral sources, A-B-C-D, etc.)

- Ability to provide a field of information as to how you met the relationship or how the contact came to know you and was entered into the database.
- Ability to track and profile personal information and preferences to build and enhance the relationship (birthdays, spouse and family information, personal preferences, hot buttons, likes and dislikes).
- Ability to code, track and measure prospects through the sales channel and pipeline.
- Have a calendaring system to pinpoint follow-up dates, follow through and action items.
- Ability to make notes on items of importance to build and connect with relationships over time.
- Ability to group and categorize contacts into other sections that allow you to customize your communication to an array of groups and associations.
- Ability to set up recurring touch points to keep connected with contacts and relationships.
- Ability to keep track of referral partners and strategic alliances for referrals and connections.
- Ability to use an integrated email send system that complies with the CAN-SPAM Act for blasting out permission based email communication.

Lead Generation

Figuring out whom to enter into your Million Dollar Database™ becomes an easy question to answer: all contacts get entered into your database! Consider your contact management system and database as your "hub" to maintain all your contacts, customers, prospects, leads and connections.

The key to effective management of your database is to make sure you have a global system in how your contacts and relationships are organized. You need a global system so you know how to sort, segment and find your key relationships by group and/or by segments. Through each of the following chapters I'm going to give you a methodology and system to organizing and categorizing your Million Dollar Database™.

One key field you'll need to track and enter data into with your Million Dollar Database™ is a field I call "How Met." How the contact came to be in your database can prove quite valuable to you over time. Knowing where you met and/or came in contact with a key relationship is something that you'll want to know as the more contacts and relationships you have in your database, the more important it is to know how a person came to know you.

Think of your database as the "hub," the central place where contacts get loaded and entered from:
- Your existing customer list(s)
- Leads from trade shows and expos
- Contacts from membership lists and directories
- Networking contacts
- Vendors and key suppliers
- Online leads from your web site
- Phone inquiries & leads
- Referral sources and strategic alliances
- Any contact worthy of keeping in touch with
- Contacts of former colleagues, bosses, coworkers, friends and associates
- Cold contacts and lists
- Lists that you've purchased from a list source

- Contacts you'd like to know more or get to know that you haven't officially met yet

Information is Power

The old saying that "Information is Power" becomes very relevant to building a Million Dollar Database™. Your database allows you the opportunity to sort and search for contacts quickly and efficiently. If you're always searching and hunting for contacts or looking for phone numbers, addresses or email addresses in different places, your database becomes your one central tool and hub of information to find contact data and information easily and quickly.

You may want to sort and search by different criteria and your database should allow you to do a sort of many fields of information, beyond name, address or phone number. What if you wanted to do a sort and find all the clients you do business with that are females? Or, what if you wanted to send a special communication to all your clients who are manufacturers in a specific zip code? Does your current system allow you the flexibility to sort and search quickly and efficiently by different sorting criteria and features?

Access to information becomes one of the main advantages to having a Million Dollar Database™. In later chapters, I'll give you a list of categories that you'll want to set up in your database so you can efficiently and quickly sort and find contacts and relationship information. The power of this information will allow you to work smarter, not harder in gaining new business, repeat business and referrals. If I told you that you could bring in 20% more business than you could before by segmenting and sorting your key contacts and relationships, would you want to read on? That's what I'm saying, so read on!

In addition, the ability to sort and search for fields of information allow you to analyze your contacts and relationships to show where you are most successful in gaining new customers. This also helps you to use the statistics that tell you who your most important client relationships are by characteristics. This allows you to spend your time on relationships that are most productive and valuable to you and your business.

Changes to Your Hub

The database system you choose today might not be the database that serves your needs in the long run. The key is to start with a database system today and know that as you get more sophisticated with needs, data, tracking, sorting and profiling information and intelligence, your needs for a database and what it can do will change. In other words, your needs will change as you start building your Million Dollar Database™. If you choose any of the systems I mentioned earlier in this chapter, it should be an easy process to export your data and migrate to another system as your needs change over time. Be willing to acknowledge that you may need a different system as your business and/or profession grows and you start to see how powerful the ability to have access to information becomes in reference to your contacts and relationships.

Your Biggest Challenge

The biggest challenge to building a Million Dollar Database™ is what I hear over and over by professionals in all types of companies and positions. The hardest part is just getting the contacts into the system, as no one has time to sit and key in data every day and code information into a computer program, right?! Who of us has more time for repetitive and computer type tasks?!

Look at this a different way, and if I told you that coding and entering your data about your key contacts and relationships could help you gain new and repeat business more effectively by as much as 20% or more, would you do it? In addition, what if using the database as your one central tool to gain better business results could lead you to capture 30% or more business and opportunity, would this be important to you?! I hope so!

If increasing your results by 20% to 30% or more doesn't work to convince you, this becomes a dilemma. If you don't see the power of how access to information about your contacts can benefit you and your business, you'll never do the next steps I recommend to building a Million Dollar Database™. You can stop reading right now, because in the next chapters I'll share how to set up, manage and benefit from your Million Dollar Database™.

If priceless relationships are important to you, your business and professional success, you'll find the resource or find the time to get contacts entered and coded into your database.

What makes managing the database and entering information so critical is that without the information in the database, you can't build a million dollars worth of opportunity or connections. Make a commitment right now to set time or assign to an assistant or hire someone to help enter and manage your contact information. If you won't make the time, then pay someone and dedicate resources to getting information in the database so you can benefit in keeping connected with your important relationships. The key here is that you have to be organized in what you want entered into the system and how you want things coded.

Think about setting up a master layout of fields to track and enter information you have on your contacts and relationships. At The Corporate Basket, we used to have a part-time dedicated staff person who regularly did data entry on new customers, prospects and contact relationships. The database became our one-stop shop to enter, track, categorize and add information. After this step, we were able to stay connected with our relationships and take time to get to know people beyond customer number, name or phone number. Slowly and strategically we gathered information about the people we did business with so we could "wow" them to set ourselves apart from all our competitors who didn't take time to gather, track and use this information. This helped us build priceless, loyal customer relationships, along with extremely loyal referral partners and strategic alliances. Read on, as the next chapters will show you how to lay out your database and what to gather, track and collect about your key relationships.

5

The Relationship Coding and Rating System (RCRS)

"Adopt a Relationship Strategy"

Organizing Your Relationships

At the center of building a Million Dollar Database™ are relationship categories you code into your database. Think about the groups and/or titles of your important business relationships. How do you define and describe your important business relationships? For most business professionals, categories like customers, loyal clients, prospects, suspects, qualified leads, referral sources, strategic alliances, other business partners, suppliers, vendors, important business contacts or influential relationships might be high on the list of categories. In addition, other relationships of importance to code and/or categorize might be former colleagues, co-workers, friends, bosses, contacts and past business relationships to maintain contact with. If you work for someone else and are looking for career connections, you might code and categorize according to type of industry and/or position or person of influence.

Ask yourself what categories you define as key relationships. Start to think in terms of coding and categorizing your contacts and key relationships so you communicate more efficiently with existing customers versus prospects. Coding and categorizing allows you to step up communication with your best customers as opposed to the one project client relationships.

All Relationships Are Not Created Equal

Building your Million Dollar Database™ is about working smarter in staying connected with your key relationships and contacts. Are all your relationships the same in terms of importance and/or influence? If you're being honest with yourself, probably not. All relationships are not created equal and you must give a rating and hierarchy to all your business relationships. We used to have a rating system at The Corporate Basket and this single tool was one of the most definitive steps I used in maintaining connections with our most important and priceless relationships. Think about this, not every customer is the same in terms of importance to you and your business or portfolio. In addition, all prospects are not the same either. Some prospects have higher potential than others, and how you keep track of which ones are more important than others can be the difference between success or failure in maintaining client relationships and closing more business.

Give a rating system to all your key contacts and relationships. Think in terms of good, better and best. Or think in terms of A's, B's, and C's to define which relationships have the highest importance to you and your business portfolio. The difference here is that you've got to define what the best relationship means to you and your portfolio as opposed to less important relationships. You've got to define what A's, B's, and C's mean. In the next few sections I outline coding and rating suggestions for your key relationship categories.

Customer Relationships

The people you do business with are most likely the most important category of relationships you have. Ask yourself how often you keep connected with each and every customer? A better question is, *should* you keep connected with each and every customer?

Rate and code your customers into a hierarchy of the most important to the least important. This is a critical step for building a Million Dollar Database™. Segment your customers into the following hierarchy of categories; A, B, C & D Customers. Think in terms of good, better, best and dud descriptor categories. You don't have to call them A's or B's, and I personally think it's a good idea to call your relationships something that makes sense to you and your business. In my company, we used to use MVP's as our most important client category. Some categories are rated as Good, Better, Best or something else that determines the ranking and hierarchy. Some people use bronze, silver and gold categories. The key is to make sure you know what each level means.

"A" Customer Relationships
These relationships are your most valuable customer relationships. The "A" customers require your time, attention and resources, and justly so. When you think of rating these

customers in your database, you'll typically find that these customers are 20% of your client relationships who provide 80% or more of your sales and revenue. "A" customer relationships are the best-of-the-best and you should give description as to how you define this type of customer. The key factor that makes this client an "A" customer is - if one of these relationships suddenly went away, this customer would have a significant impact to you and your business portfolio. These customers are low in number but high in dollars, sales and/or profitability, which make them extremely important to your client portfolio. Things like sales volume, longevity of business relationship, lifetime value of the relationship along with the services and/or products purchased make this client an MVP (most valuable person) to you and your business portfolio. On another note, these customer relationships should be profiled, as they take time and attention to nurture. These relationships can take your time and attention away from your "B" customers, your bread and butter accounts. One of the most important reasons to code "A" relationships is that you should spend a great amount of time, attention and resources on them as they make up 80% of your portfolio.

The danger zone is that most professionals do spend their time with "A" customer relationships and forget about the other key relationships and the hidden potential they have for repeat and continued business and referrals.

"B" Customer Relationships
These relationships are typically your bread and butter account relationships. Most likely to account for 35% of your total clients, this category of business is typically your most loyal customer relationships. Due to the fact

most professionals spend their time with "A" customer relationships, your "B" customers don't get the time and attention they deserve and you miss the boat in gaining repeat business and referrals from this category of relationship. Your bread and butter accounts are repeat customers who use your services and/or buy your products over and over again. They may not be your highest volume customers, but when you look at how loyal they are and how they account to the overall sales of your business or portfolio, they are typically the customers who allow you to keep the lights on and the bills paid. The biggest opportunity with these customers is to take care of them due to their loyalty and ask for referrals from them as they are your happy, satisfied and loyal customer base. These are the customers to ask for referrals and introductions to if you keep connected and communicate with them regularly! These are the customer relationships that typically fall by the wayside due to neglect and indifference. Make a commitment today to let them know of their value to you and your business. Don't miss the opportunity to stay connected with these key customers!

"C" Customer Relationships

Your "C" relationships are typically what I call the one shot wonders. These are your one time accounts and typically the lower accounts or projects in sales and volume. These customers account for about 45% of your customer list and have high potential to move into a higher volume, more productive and valuable relationship. These are the customers that you want to communicate with at a more frequent level to uncover needs and see what must be done in getting them to work with you over and over again. In most companies, these are the forgotten customer relationships because their lower volume and account level get lost in the midst of more important, higher volume account relationships. Most professionals don't feel there is enough time to work with and take care of these relationships. These customers typically leave or go elsewhere due to feeling unappreciated, neglected and being treated indifferently as to importance. Two thirds of these customers walk away because they lack nurturing and attention. If you segment and communicate differently with your "C" customer relationships, you may convert a large number into more valuable relationships by spending quality time, focused attention and brief amounts of attention with them. The key is to not let these relationships slip away.

"D" Customer Relationships
These are your "undesirable" customer relationships. While I'm sure every customer is important to you and your business, there are some customers that, if evaluated, you would rethink the value they bring as a customer relationship. These customers are not the best fit in working together with you over the long run. While you may not stop being of service to these customers, these relationships get less time and attention than the more loyal, valuable client relationships. This category of relationship is important to pay attention to as your business and customer portfolio grows. There is a time and point that these relationships may not be the best fit for you and your business and you should pay attention to the characteristics that make up this category of client relationship. This is a hard decision to make for most busy and successful professionals, as I'm not recommending you ignore this customer relationship

but I do suggest you limit the time, attention and resources you dedicate to this account relationship as your higher value relationships should command your attention and resources.

Your Ideal Client Profile
Once you've given thought to the rating of your customer relationships, keep an updated Ideal Client Profile on file to make sure you're rating your customer relationships at least once a year. Customer relationships change over time and you want to make sure you're paying attention to who your good, better and best customers are in your portfolio (See Appendix A).

Relationship Rating System and Benefits

The main benefit to giving a rating to your customer relationships is that you see how to work more effectively in gaining new customers. This rating system allows you to communicate more strategically in staying connected to your good, better and best client relationships. In a later chapter, I'll talk about communication strategies that give you the best bang for your buck with each level of customer category.

Once you have an Ideal Client Profile completed, you now have a better road map to categorize and rate the prospects you intend to go after for new business. Along with coding your customer relationships, you can now use this information to target your prospecting efforts and rate potential customer relationships. This one strategy helped my organization bring in 25% more business to our company as we had a targeted approach to bringing in new business as opposed to "any" business will do. If you're looking to be more effective in how you bring in new business, this next section is an important part to pay close attention to.

Potential Customer Relationships

Potential Customers
Setting up a prospecting and sales system in your database for acquiring new business is an ongoing challenge for sales professionals. Not every prospect is the same in terms of high potential and likelihood of gaining their business. Also, keeping track of who is a more likely prospect than others is always a challenge to track and monitor for follow-up and results.

One thing you must do is develop an Ideal Prospect Profile (Appendix B) to make sure you're working smart to go after new business. Think of giving a similar rating to your prospects as you did to your customer relationships. From cold prospects to hot leads, your Million Dollar Database™ is how you give a ranking and hierarchy to the potential of each lead and prospect.

Giving a relationship rating to potential customers and prospects is how you'll begin to develop a pipeline and prospecting system that helps prioritize those most likely to do business with you in the long run. Most sales programs teach you to "pitch and run." Pitch 'em with your message and then run away if they don't buy from you right then and there. Think of your potential customers as a ladder that gradually moves upward from cold prospect, to suspect, to hot qualified lead, to eventual customer based on your Million Dollar Database™ relationship rating system.

"C" - Prospects as Potential Customers

Prospect relationships are the coldest of potential customer relationships. Typically, these relationships are entered into your database as cold leads. Prospects might be entered into your database from directories, lists or associations. You may have met one of these contacts at a special event or networking meeting. For some sales professionals, these contacts may also come from cold calling and entering business card information into the database. The key description of this kind of relationship is that they are unqualified and need to have more information provided in order to move up the potential customer rating system. Code these relationships as prospects until you gather and glean more information about their potential for you and your services or products.

"B" - Suspects as Potential Customers

These relationships are converted from prospect relationships to suspects at the time you have gathered, received information and/or acquired information that might suggest interest in your products or services. These contacts have, either through interest, inquiry or information shown promise or potential for your goods or services. It's important that this relationship category move up one step along the ladder to potential customer status. Typically, suspects get lost in tracking and follow-up because most sales professionals and businesses lose touch with this contact as there's no system to continue to "woo" and follow-up at this level. This contact has potential, but most sales professionals and businesses focus on the hot prospects that need attention now. This category becomes important to maintain communication with, as the right follow-up may convert these relationships into qualified leads and customers in the long run.

"A" - Qualified Leads as Potential Customers
The qualified lead is one step removed from being a customer relationship. This contact moves up the ladder from suspect to qualified lead when there's a qualifying trigger event, situation or type of intelligence that qualifies this potential customer as most likely to buy in the near future. This contact becomes high on your follow-up lead list to close at a certain point in the future in consideration of your products or services. Losing touch with this level of contact can prove devastating to you and your business because this is a hot lead that needs your time, attention and follow-up to gain new business! Don't let this contact be lost through lack of follow through, communication and attention needed to gain this new customer!

Ideal Prospect Profile
Once you've identified the potential customer categories and hierarchy, you can develop an Ideal Prospect Profile (See Appendix B) to keep focused on the rating and description of prospects versus suspects versus qualified lead status. Having a system of prospecting in this manner will help you develop the processes you've been missing in organization from your database. In a later chapter I'll be sharing how to communicate differently with each of these categories of potential customers.

Each segment has a different goal associated with it to convert cold prospects into paying customers by using your database as the central tool in prospecting, coding, tracking and follow through. Just imagine the new business you'll gain by moving potential customers through your new sales prospecting system. The end result is a seamless and organized system to gain new business through your Million Dollar Database™!

Referral Relationships

Relationships that provide referrals are a forgotten category in the database of many business professionals. Most of us want to acknowledge our best referral sources and strategic alliances, but a system in how to keep track of referrals escapes us. To build a Million Dollar Database™ is to keep track of those who refer you business regularly and set up a rating system for those who might refer to you with consistent and regular communication.

Referral Partners and Strategic Alliances

Referral partners and strategic alliances are a very important relationship category. This category of business partner is a two-way street to opportunities and connections. Referral partners are those types of businesses or individuals who most compliment you and your business and who serve a similar target market. These contacts need to be coded and communicated with to build a solid stream of referrals and new opportunities. You should surround yourself with these powerful referral partners as this relationship category can be your best roving sales force to search out opportunity and alert you to hot prospects ready to purchase now.

The question becomes, how well do you keep connected with these powerful referral partners and strategic alliances? With your database coded into a similar hierarchy as your prospect and customer relationships, you're now able to build the relationships with those who send you business the most and communicate more strategically with those who might have potential to send you business in the future. Now that's something of value to you and your business, right?!

"A" Referral Partners & Strategic Alliances
Those referral partners who have consistently sent you business more than once and have shown huge loyalty in talking you up to other people that resulted in business are a critical category and relationship. Take care of these relationships as these are your most valued referral partners! Just like your customer relationships, you'll want to communicate and interact more frequently with this category of referral partner as they have shown through their actions that they believe in who you are and have referred business to you more than once! This relationship needs attention and nurturing to continue sending business your way! Reward these loyal referral partners with appreciation and your time to show how valued the relationship is.

"B" Referral Partners & Strategic Alliances
Referral partners who have attempted to send you business and referrals or those who have introduced you to opportunity once as a referral relationship are important as a category. These partnerships should be coded accordingly as these relationships need nurturing, attention and education so you receive the right kind of introductions to new business and opportunities. This area is where I see most professionals go wrong in assuming referral partners and strategic alliances automatically know how to make an introduction or referral. Using your Million Dollar

Database™ effectively is to interact and educate these referral partners with situations to look for and what key questions or phrases they can ask on your behalf to refer business opportunity to you. Education is your key strategy here so that those who might refer to you actually send you solid-gold opportunities.

"C" Referral Partners & Strategic Alliances
We all have a number of contacts and relationships that might be potential referral partners, but the challenge always becomes how to build a partnership with these contacts and improve the trust and like factor so that efforts are made by these relationships to send you introductions. "Might-refer" can easily turn into "will-refer" if you take the time needed to meet with these potential referral partners and get to know them and build trust and respect with them. People refer business to people they know, they like and they trust. Code these relationships and look at meeting with them and interacting with them to build this partnership and you will find more referrals come your way than ever before! Just as you need to get to know a prospect and uncover opportunities, the same holds true with potential referral partners and strategic alliances.

Change your business strategy now to dedicate time to follow-up and communicate with your best and highest potential referral partners just like you do in dedicating time to take care of your existing customers relationships and high potential prospects. Change your game and change your results! I personally experienced an increase in new business through referrals by as much as 15% in one year by implementing this very strategy!

You've Gotta Give to Get
One note I'd like to make on building referral partners and strategic alliances is that this category of relationship typically works most effectively if you 'give' before you 'get.' What I mean is, if you're spending as much time offering to be a resource as often as you're trying to gain referrals and introductions, you'll be much more successful when you make the effort to give first before you try and get. I don't know many successful business professionals who can rely solely on "getting" referrals without offering to be a resource first. So the strategy becomes 'give' first to provide value and opportunity and then you'll find the 'get.'

Key Questions – Trigger Events – When to Refer
A challenge I've experienced in the past while building solid referral partners and strategic alliances is how to keep track of what your referral partners want and who to refer them to. In your Million Dollar Database™ you should have a section that allows you to keep track of the businesses and/or consumers to send your referral partners to. In addition, I've always found it helpful to have a set of key questions to ask or situations to look for, or trigger event to watch out for that tells you when to make the referral or introduction.

Other Key Relationship Categories

Other key relationship categories important to you and your business might be:

Supplier & Vendor Relationships
Those businesses and professionals you buy from or use the services of are important relationships to maintain

communication with. Ready access to vendor information along with who the good, better and best vendors are can be valuable information to have access to. At The Corporate Basket, I found it important to source our suppliers through our database system when we needed products quick and fast and couldn't get them from our main suppliers. Ready access along with building relationships with our key suppliers proved invaluable when we needed products and/or services quickly and faster than the normal turnaround.

Former Colleagues, Co-Workers & Classmates

Keeping in contact with those professionals and/or colleagues you used to work with or know can be quite valuable to you at some point in your future. If you need to call in a favor, find a connection, receive an introduction, or need a resource, those you used to work with may be the differentiator between success and failure. Don't let former colleagues and associates slip away. Keep connected and stay in touch.

Former Bosses

Wow, do I actually need to describe the value of this category?! Have you ever needed a reference for a potential career connection or reference from any previous employer?! Good relationships with former bosses and superiors are a very good thing! Send a card once in awhile or better yet, know their birthday and send a well-timed card for the important day. Trust me, you don't want to lose touch with those you used to report to and work with. These contacts and relationships have helped me in many situations over the years beyond using my former bosses as references. Keep in touch and don't burn bridges!

Former Business Associates

When I left the banking industry and started my own business, I found the business professionals I had built relationships with during my banking career critical to my success in starting my own business. I was rewarded with helpful professionals who provided services, resources and information in the launch and start of my business venture. Without these wonderful relationships I would have had to pay for and collect information that might have taken me years to find and afford.

With the relationships I had built over the years, my launch in business was built on solid resources and business partners and providers. Many of these business professionals I continue to work with today, almost 17 years later. The message: Never lose touch with former business associates. Guess who the professionals are that I refer business to today when I hear one of my clients or current business associates mention a need for professional services or resources? Yep, you guessed it! Now I refer to those that helped me in my start in business. I'm a great resource to them! Ask yourself how much of a resource you are to your business associates and colleagues. If you don't give on occasion, you won't get.....trust me!

Peers & Colleagues

Finding new business partners and colleagues is always a work in progress. People come and go but relationships should be for a lifetime. The problem is people don't stay in touch on a regular basis. Just imagine how much more successful you'd be if you just took the time to communicate and stay in touch with your current peers and colleagues. I'm not talking about constant communication, but more than a cursory holiday card each year. You never know when a peer or colleague might prove to be a valuable resource to you or those you know who need information or resources.

Executive Assistant and the Administrative Professional
Books have been written on this subject alone as to the importance of gaining access to busy executives through their assistant. Tracking the administrative aide to an executive or CEO and getting to know them through association and communication may be the difference between gaining access and landing new business accounts or not. I always found it helpful to track the assistant's name in association with the executive, so I could get to know the assistant, and any details I could glean from the administrative professional about their boss.

Competitors & Enemies
What's the phrase we all know well from the movie, The Godfather? "Keep your friends close, but your enemies closer"? If you own your own business, you need to keep on top of who your competitors are and what they're up to. If you have enemies in business (and we all do) you should keep your enemies on the radar to watch and observe and pay attention. Flag a specific section in your database for competitors and enemies. Keep up on what they're doing. Stay in communication, not to build a relationship but to glean information, knowledge and a competitive edge. Need I say more?

Persons of Influence
Key persons of influence in the community – do you know them or wish you knew them? Track and ask for introductions

to persons of influence if they make sense to you and your business. You need to know who you want to know before someone can open a door for you. I've always believed in the saying "If you don't ask, you don't get." Keep track of who you'd like to know and ask for introductions and referrals to meet these persons of influence.

Contacts Not Assigned
Sometimes you meet people and you don't know upfront their potential to you and your business. These contacts are good to flag as not assigned and keep them segmented for some future opportunity and/or need.

Contacts You'd Like to Know
When reading a magazine or listening to the news, if you hear about someone locally or nationally that you'd like to know, flag this person in your database as a future contact of influence. I've found it effective to follow-up with those I wanted to meet and try to get to know them through a series of "saw you in the news" or notes how I enjoyed what they discussed in the media. People like to know they've been seen and heard, so communicating with those power leaders and/or local persons of influence can be a great way to make high-powered connections in your community. I've sent copies of the articles to those I'd like to introduce myself to and know better. The only way I found to organize getting to know someone I didn't know was through my Million Dollar Database™ to code and track all the interactions and notes I could about the individual until I finally got the chance to meet them. Once I met them and/or had an introduction, I now had the opportunity to stay connected and keep in touch with them.

Former Friends
You never know when you might want to reconnect and/or re-engage with friends you've lost touch with or those that you've lost friendships with. Good to keep them flagged as I've reconnected with many former friends. Life just seems to keep you apart, but then something occurs and you find you'd like to reconnect again.

How Much is Too Much

While coding relationships can be unlimited in category, every business and portfolio is different and you should give thought to the categories that make most sense to your business portfolio. I've found it so much easier to code categories of relationships so I can customize and zip out targeted communication. Staying in touch with my former bosses and colleagues is a much different type of communication and message than how I keep connected to customer relationships. The main difference is to think about the goal of the message. For clients, I'm looking to keep connected for repeat and referral business. For colleagues and former business associates I'm looking to stay in touch as much for the referrals as I am for the ongoing bond of our continued association. Sometimes it's effective just to stay in touch for the benefit of staying in touch! In later chapters I'll give you wonderful examples of strategies to strengthen the bond through communication with all your different relationship categories.

Other Fields to Track

In addition to coding and giving a hierarchy to your categories of relationships, it's important to track other details and information on your contacts. Many times, you might find it important to sort and search for common characteristics about key relationships. Without having details noted in your database from the beginning, this function becomes either a challenge or an easy process, depending on what information you gather about your key contacts and relationships as you learn information about them over time.

Think today about the information you wish you knew about your contacts and relationships so you could work smarter and go after the right kind of business as opposed to any kind of business. Whether someone is a homeowner or renter, male or female, over 60 years of age or fewer than 21, think what you would like to know about your contacts. Tracking the common characteristics of your relationships that, when analyzed, provides you valuable information about where to target your efforts to gain future business and/or repeat business is effective in gaining a competitive edge. I'm a big believer that information is power, so long as it helps you be more targeted and more efficient with your efforts to do better business.

How Met
I have always found it extremely useful to know how I actually met a contact or key relationship. With customers, it's critical as I can sort and then analyze where my best customers have come to be, either through a few key referral partners, success from a particular industry association, trade show, or through web site inquiries and leads that have converted into paying customers. How great would it be for you to know exactly where you gain your best business

from and be able to search and sort for this information with the click of a few keys in your Million Dollar Database™?!

You should have a section or field in your database to know how you met a key contact and relationship. By having this section in your database, it's a handy reference tool whenever you want to show how well you remember details and remind people where you met each other originally. This is also an effective measurement tool to track where you've met your best referral sources and/or clients. Knowing how your contacts came to be in your database is a key section to flag and track. Trust me, you'll impress and get some "ooh's and aah's" for remembering this little gem of information as you build relationships with those in your database!

Contact Title or Function

The title and/or function of the person you have in your database are other fields to track data on if you sell to businesses. If you want to sort and send out communication to all the Human Resources Directors, CEO's or CFO's in your database, or any other title or function, this field helps you target your communication and message to the needs of this company representative by title and/or function within a company.

Size of Company

Selling products or services to companies creates a need to track the size of the company you do business with and target for future business. By tracking the size of the company, and having a series of fields to select from in reference to size by revenue or employee size, you're able to profile and track the characteristics of your best clients and describe this characteristic to your referral sources in how to refer the right size company and opportunity to you.

Type of Company

For my business, I always paid close attention to the type of company we gained business from. Whether it was insurance companies, commercial banks, law firms or realtors, I wanted to know what type of company and organization we did business with the most. By sorting our client relationships and customizing our communication to the different needs of these special industries, we were able to set ourselves apart and showcase our products and services to fit the individual needs relative to the industry we served.

Male / Female

How about knowing how much of your business comes from whether individuals are male or female? To some of you, this field of information makes no sense at all to track. But to some of you, especially those who sell products or services to individuals, this field might be critical, along with the age of the individuals of your client relationships. I work with professionals who rely on knowing the gender of their contacts, so their database tracking is critical to have the ability to sort by a gender specified field. You have to make the decision as to what's an important field to track for you and your database, as these are only a few ideas and/or categories you might want to track specifically.

Email Marketing – Y/N

We do business in a digital world and by having the ability to code contacts to receive and/or not receive email marketing and promotions are critical today. Do you have the ability to code communication on or off, depending on how your relationships want you to communicate with them? You should have a field to flag whether or not people receive email communication from you. Now, some of you are thinking that your email service provider does this on its own when your contacts unsubscribe from your email communication, however, you'll want to hard code this request in your database on your own.

At The Corporate Basket we used to take this one step further and when contacts of ours wanted to unsubscribe from communications via email, we would acknowledge the request and then ask the contact if they wanted us to send them one of our printed catalogs. We were happy to honor their request of not communicating via email with them in the future. We also asked if there was an opportunity for us to step up and be of service in the future by packaging any sort of appreciation gifts and if we could make a personal visit to meet with them. If you only knew the thousands of dollars worth of business we used to rack up with this little strategy! We used a process that, for most companies, was a dead end in opportunity. We converted this request into new business and revenue, simply by having a process through our database to communicate differently with those who chose not to receive email marketing from us. This was successful for us in gaining new business and one that I hope you get ideas from with your relationships.

Some people just don't want to receive communication via email today, as they're overloaded with too much promotion in their inbox. By taking a more relationship-centered approach to contacting potential customers, we captured tons of business. Ask yourself what kind of business you could gain if you paid a little closer attention to the small details to relate on a more personal level with those who might buy from you or do business with you again. Email marketing is great for efficiency, but not so great to build the personal touch in relations or communication. The best results today in email marketing are those series of communication where the email message is personalized to the individual receiving the email. The blast email marketing not personalized is quickly becoming ineffective for relationship building. Please don't misunderstand me, I'm not saying that email marketing can't be effective. In a later chapter, I'll talk about the strategies to use when communicating with email marketing and what the difference should be in your goals to communicate and whether you personalize the communication.

And the List of Categories Goes On and On
Other categories you might want to think about are categories like groups or associations, age and income level, homeowners or renters, type of commercial location, and the types of services and/or products purchased from you. These categories are important if they make sense to track in your database and with your portfolio of contacts. The key is to think about what to track so you have more information that helps you do better business.

Maintenance Is Key
Most businesses and professionals want to code their contacts and relationships better. The challenge becomes in the management of the database and how to keep contacts up-to-date and organized in your Million Dollar Database™.

This is where you need to think about how important this information could be to you and your business. I don't change anything for my business unless I can understand how I'll benefit from implementing something that on the front end seems like more work. You need to be a visionary here and see that, in the long run, you'll love the benefits tracking and coding will bring to you and your portfolio when you're looking to reach out and stay connected with your best contacts and relationships. Again, if I told you that you'll land more repeat business and gain more referrals from your existing contacts and relationships, wouldn't you want to change some things in your business and how you do what you do? The big payoff is down the road if you'll see it by changing what you code and track about your key relationships.

Stick with me, as in the next few chapters I'll discuss how to benefit from all the tracking and coding. Tracking and coding is only the beginning, as with new information comes new power. The next question to ask yourself is, "How well do you know your contacts both personally and professionally?" The more you know about your contacts and how you glean this information is the next step to building a Million Dollar Database™.

How Well Dost' Thou Know Thee

"Pay Attention To The Details"

Sweat The Small Stuff

The next step in Building a Million Dollar Database™ centers on the premise there's power in who you know and how well you know them! You need to sweat the small stuff and pay attention to what your contacts say and do, and what things matter most to them. It's important to use your database as the central tracking tool to gather intelligence and information about your important contacts and relationships.

The Hidden Gold Mine - Intelligence Gathering

Some professionals have asked me at my workshops and seminars why gathering intelligence is important to success in business. The answer: If relationships are central to helping you be more successful in dealing with people in your profession, then what you know about your contacts can be a defining measurement as to the success, or lack of, you have in business.

When you find out what your key relationships like, don't like, what matters to them, are of importance to them and what common interests you may have with them, this gives you the building blocks on which to build priceless relationships. This also gives you the opportunity to step up and provide your services or products in a manner such that you compete with no one.

Priceless relationships equal loyalty. People do business and refer business to those they like and trust. The more someone knows you and the more you know about them, the more chances you have to set yourself apart. Building loyal, priceless relationships over time can pay off in so many ways beyond just purchasing goods and services. Connections, favors, advancement, repeat business, access to information and introductions to persons of influence happen when you know your relationships well.

Good Versus Evil

There's a corrupt side to gathering business intelligence. The strategies suggested in this book are to be used for positive business intelligence, not evil intelligence gathering. There is a dark side to gleaning information on people, where what you know can be used against someone. I want you to think about only the good side, the side where what you know about people is a strategy so important that your contacts only think of you when you need connections, referrals, introductions and information, in addition to orders for services or products.

Business intelligence gathering is used as a strategy to gather information about the people you do business with and would like to do business with so you get to know them. By knowing them well you are in a position to ask for and get things you never could unless you know someone really well. It's the reason people buy today. It's the reason information is shared. It's why people recommend and endorse others for career positions, jobs, board positions or coveted assignments. Every consumer and organization has too many choices of what to buy when they seek products and services today. Getting to know someone and having a strong relationship means that when the decision to use products or services, refer someone for future business, provide an introduction for a position or recommend or endorse you over other choices, the answer becomes how well you know the person you're relying on to provide that favor or connection.

So, if I've ranted enough about the power of knowing your contacts and key relationships, how do you go about gathering intelligence and then use this powerful information to get connections, favors, new business, referrals and/or access to information?

"Intel" Gathering

What to gather on your key relationships is another business strategy that goes back to your key relationships and categories. I've been asked in presentations as to what 'intelligence' means? Intelligence, or 'intel,' is information that can't typically be found in a list or report or web site. 'Intel' is gathered by a series of interactive questions and discovery to get to know your key relationships and find out what that person likes, what they enjoy, their personal family information, business intelligence, personal background, hometown information, what floats their boat and what they care about so that you can track the information and use this 'intel' to build a more personalized relationship with that individual. This is the ultimate strategy in how to set you apart. This 'intel' gathering sets you apart from all the array of businesses and professionals who never get to know a person beyond customer number, name, address, phone number and email. It's also the main strategy for why you won't have to work so hard at trying to get people to buy from you or provide you introductions. The more you have a solid relationship with someone, the less you'll have to ask for the business, because you'll get the business many times without having to ask for it!

Your job in building a Million Dollar Database™ is to start slowly and strategically gathering needed information to profile and gain intelligence on your relationships and use the information as a communication tool to send something, or do something, to delight those that you know. It all boils down to providing some sort of communication or experience that shows you've paid attention, taken the time to make contact, and showcase that you know the person well.

Peel an Onion

Like an onion, people and relationships have lots of layers and to get to know your key relationships and contacts takes time, strategy and patience. The goal of gathering intelligence is to get to know what people like, what they need and what they're all about so as to track and profile information and communicate in such a way as your relationships think you know them better than they know themselves.

Through a series of interactions you experience with your key contacts, you collect information and log it away for future reference. You need to be organized and at the ready to ask questions and converse in such a way as to gather information without someone knowing what you're up to. People reveal their true identity and preferences over time so your goal in gathering intelligence is to learn about your relationships slowly and strategically through conversation and communication. Your goal is to uncover opportunity and information through phone interactions, via email, in face-to-face interaction and anytime you have the opportunity to converse with your relationships.

In later chapters, I'll explain methods in how to communicate with the intelligence you've gathered to build priceless relationships in your Million Dollar Database™. For this chapter, let's talk about the intelligence you should be gathering about your relationships.

Interrogation – Not!

For almost 17 years I've been collecting intelligence on my best business relationships and I can tell you emphatically that interrogating your contacts to get them to provide personal and business information is NOT what I'm talking about. You can't gather intelligence quickly or all at once. The hardest part of collecting intelligence on your key relationships is how to conduct this over time and to be organized about gathering data so you can use this information in the future.

You need to think of yourself as a secret intelligence agent gathering information. Anytime you interact with a contact, you strategically ask your best relationships a series of questions over time to collect personal information like birthday information, family information, business information, what they care about and what their preferences are.

You notice things, you hear things, and you ask questions and gather data in such a way as the other party may not notice you collecting information. You log this information into your database to be used in the future for communicating and standing out to show you noticed and that you care. Now begs the question: What intelligence should you collect and gather on your important business relationships?

Business & Professional Information

Knowing as much as you can about the professional and their business is important. Collect information about the person's business career and company history, how long have they been in their profession or industry, their educational background, military background, what do they like most about what they do, what are they proudest of, what kinds of associations do they belong to, what accomplishments have they achieved or been awarded? This information is gathered through conversation and over time, not through a series of questions you interview someone with. How you gather information is as important as what you gather on your relationships.

The best way to gather this data is through relaxed conversation over lunch, dinner, cocktails or breakfast. This isn't the information you try to gather over the phone or via email. As we go forward in this chapter, some information gathering techniques lend themselves to being captured via phone or email, and other information needs to be collected in a relaxed, more social environment where people share more personal and/or private information with you.

As you first meet someone and get to know them, you can gather normal business intelligence like length of time in business, how long the company has been in existence, how many employees, their position and other key business statistics. This information is OK to collect in more of an interview type setting.

If you're trying to get to know a prospect better, the administrative assistant can provide effective business information about a person's likes, dislikes, business information, etc. The key is how you go about collecting the information to then use it.

Sweat the Small Stuff – Gain Big Results
I had a client years ago who was trying to "woo" a new prospect into converting their entire banking relationship over to their financial institution. This prospect was one of the "big fish" known in the manufacturing community and my client had been trying to get information about this client for quite awhile, but nothing proved valuable to use in converting the prospect over to working with my banker client, Jim.

Jim paid attention and logged information over time about the company and clients this company served, what their products and services were, how long the company had been in business, how many employees, etc. He had met with the CEO and had lunch to gather more personal bits of information and business type information about the CEO and what he was interested in. For personal information and hobbies, the CEO liked basketball and he happened to be a golf nut. He even got to know the assistant to the CEO extremely well but found nothing that could be used to set himself apart to "woo" the relationship.

After spending almost six months logging information in about this prospect and maintaining contact with the CEO fairly frequently, it seemed like nothing would crack the relationship code in finding a way to really "woo" the relationship over for Jim. The CEO and Jim had actually built a somewhat social relationship, so Jim went back frequently to the database intelligence to update information about the manufacturing business. On one frequent occasion, Jim noticed the company history and information. He had logged in some time ago how long this manufacturing business had been around. Jim noticed that the company he was trying to bring into the bank was coming up on their 10 year anniversary in business.

Jim set out to have a "congratulations" celebration delivered to the company on their 10 year anniversary date. He also worked back with the assistant who provided him the company logo to have a plaque made up with a 10 year anniversary seal for the company's name and corporate identity engraved on it.

On the anniversary date, Jim, along with a few delivery helpers arrived at the company to deliver the 10 year Anniversary party. Needless to say, Jim so thoroughly delighted the company CEO that he not only landed the $10M business account of the manufacturer, but also got introductions to four of the key suppliers that the manufacturing firm used. Here lies the perfect example of how important information may be to you in the future. Had Jim not paid attention to logging information into his database, he never would have remembered the company anniversary date. The moral to the story is, sweat the small stuff - It may pay off big time in the future!

Personal Information

Collecting personal information on people is a little easier to gather as people like to talk about themselves, so anytime you get the chance to ask people about their family, their life and their children, it's a good time to take notes and log information for future reference. Birthday information is good here and also any personal hobbies or special interests you might take note on someone.

Personal Pays Off
A client of mine, Sandy, used to send gift baskets for her customers that had a military background. Sandy would make a special note of any clients of hers who were in the military or retired from military service. Each July 4th holiday, my client would send personalized July 4th gift baskets, including special wooden boxes with the designated branch of the military that her clients served, along with a special message noting their dedication and how great our country was due to their dedication and sacrifice. The baskets were decked out as red, white and blue picnic baskets loaded with goodies and fun July 4th memorabilia for the entire family. The special gift was the commemorative wooden box with the customized seals. Sandy paid attention to

what branch of the military each client served, along with any special phrases and/or comments her clients would say about their experience in the military. She wanted to make sure and recognize those who had given so much in sacrifice to our Country. This was a "wow" factor tradition that we enjoyed packaging every year before July 4th. I always enjoyed hearing all the accolades she received in thank you's, new business, referrals and testimonials for her special, personalized gifts.

Birthday Information

I've worked with hundreds and hundreds of businesses and professionals who would like to implement a birthday program but never seem to find the right intelligence gathering method in collecting data to execute the birthday program. Most professionals find that they are willing and ready to implement a birthday program but find gathering the needed intelligence the difficulty.

At The Corporate Basket, we used to first follow-up with key customers regularly and keep in touch by asking them their favorite color and when their birthday was. We created a sort of game out of making contact and asking our clients for their birthday information. Most clients were more than willing to provide the information and when asked why we wanted their birthday, we would share that we had some fun things planned in the future for them. We rarely got turned down for the information. In the last few years of owning The Corporate Basket, we started asking clients their birthday from the first order. We made it part of the order process and it became seamless for us to collect the data.

At the end of each month I would pull a list that I sorted from our database and flagged who the customers were we would send gifts to that would receive a gift with their favorite color (the A's) and the clients and contacts we would send cards to (the B's) and the clients we would send an email birthday note to (the C's). I also flagged any special client that I hadn't met with recently or ones that I wanted to invite to a birthday lunch. There were some clients that I wanted one-to-one time with and their birthday lunch or celebration via cocktails close to their birthday was a great way to get me face to face with clients and contacts I wanted more personal contact time with. This segmenting allowed us to acknowledge the most important relationships with gifts and cards, and the others received an email birthday card or call. We received rave reviews from many of our customers for recognizing their special day. I have to admit, we benefited greatly from doing this with our clients, as many of our customers wanted to implement a similar program with their client base. The challenge was always having our clients provide their customer birthday information to us ahead of time.

So many professionals want to implement a birthday program, yet so few professionals actually take the time and work out a system to gather the information. You will be miles ahead of your competition by implementing this one key strategy. Log the birthday information in your Million Dollar Database™ by using one key field for birthday information of your clients. Implementation is as easy as sorting and clicking a button to get the information.

The Photographer and Using Birthday Information
I always look for unique examples of how people use intelligence to delight and "wow" their business relationships. Years ago I had a photographer client that looked for unique ways to delight their customers by using business intelligence. This client, Sal, was quite known for the fabulous weddings he photographed in the Southern California area. Sal had built a solid portfolio in the wedding business and for family photography.

When clients would get married, Sal would once a year send off anniversary cards to the happy couple and stay in touch with them through other life events. When Sal would get a couple who recently had a baby, Sal would log the children's information into his database and then send a very special one year birthday card, along with a discount for photography services for the child's first birthday event.

If you could only imagine the kudos' and "wow" factor the birthday cards created! This guy gets the award for unique, timely communication to stay connected with his favorite clients and relationships! What creative ideas can you come up with to keep connected and "wow" your key relationships?

Family Information

Capturing information about the spouse of a key contact and any information about their children can be valuable information to use over time. I always found it helpful in client conversations to ask how the kids were doing, or pay close attention when someone mentioned their children were graduating from high school or college. Listening for information on other personal or family information such as when a client is moving, changing jobs, getting promoted, buying or selling a home, dealing with family issues, or facing family emergencies or death can be valuable to you and your relationships. These are critical moments to pay attention to and listen for moments of opportunity to show you care and cement the relationship with kindness and personal attention.

Listen for Moments of Opportunity to Cement Solid Relationships
I once had a client that was going through a very tough time with her husband who had recently had a stroke. I happened to be in the unfortunate circumstance of going through something similar with my husband years earlier and had quite a bit of information for support with families who have a loved one who's had a stroke. I sent my client lots of web site information and copies of articles that I had collected years earlier. I still get comments about the nice touch and how helpful the information was to her. That particular client was worth thousands to me over the years, not only for direct business, but the many clients she referred to me over the years. I know that our relationship had a firm foundation because I took the time to pay attention and note her circumstance with helpful information at a personal level.

Be Sensitive to Things That Change

While it's important to collect and gather intelligence on personal information and business information of your key relationships, it's also important to remember that things change in the lives of your key relationships. People change jobs, family units change due to divorce and/or unforeseen circumstances, people have more children, lose children and you've got to pay close attention to the family and business situation your relationships are in. Log this information into your database and make a strong commitment to keep up-to-date with family and personal information. The personal connection you have and the knowledge you have on key relationships is central to building a solid bond and connection with people. This, in turn, leads to priceless relationships that result in introductions, repeat business and referrals.

The Two Biggest Secrets to Effective Intelligence Gathering

There are two big secrets to effective intelligence gathering: listening and jotting. You've got to dial in and listen for cues to bits of information shared through conversation and interaction. In addition, jotting is required to make sure the information you gather is collected and noted in your Million Dollar Database™. The more dialed in you are to listen for relationship-oriented cues the more intelligence you'll gather for use in the future. It's so easy through the normal course of interaction with your key contacts to collect good intelligence if you have a game plan in gathering the information. The key is to jot the information down on paper, or electronically, so you capture and enter this data into your database. I don't' recommend that you rely on your brain for intelligence gathering. Become a jotter and take notes during your interaction with key relationships and then enter the data into your Million Dollar Database™. The more "intel" you have on contacts, the better you can use this information to engage, relate and communicate with your relationships down the road.

Power goes to the one in the know – so ask yourself what you are doing and what you will do to collect important information going forward. To be more successful in business and build a Million Dollar Database™ means learning about your key contacts and relationships. You need to listen for cues as you interact with your relationships. You must collect data and pay attention to recognize small moments of opportunity that help you cement the relationship.

Gathering data is only half the battle, the other half is how you use the information you collect, enter into your database, and use for the future to cement a strong relationship. How you use the intelligence to keep connected and top of mind with your key contacts is the main benefit to intelligence. In the next chapter I'll discuss how to use the intelligence and benefit from the knowledge you gain and learn about your relationships.

Relationships Must be Fed & Watered

"Reach Out to People Consistently"

Nurture Your Relationships

It's not enough to have your contacts in a database if you don't use the information you've collected and gathered about them. Once your contacts are in your database and segmented and categorized, your job now is to communicate with your key contacts to bring value to the relationship and nurture those relationships into results! Plants wither and die without nurturing…as do relationships. Nurture your relationships. Keep connected with clients and referral sources. Engage and be interested in who people are and what they're all about. Look for critical moments of opportunity to maintain the personal connection and bond. The more you believe this and exhibit this in your business model, the more results you'll see through relationships to new business, opportunities, repeat business, favors, connections and resources.

Whether your goal is to "woo" new customers, build repeat business from your existing client relationships, gain connections, favors or build better loyalty and referrals, your success depends on nurturing your key relationships into opportunity and results. If you've started to gather intelligence on your key relationships, you can now set out with a game plan to stay connected to produce results!

It's Business – And Yes, It's Personal

The reason you've gathered intelligence is to make the relationship more personal in nature. The more personal you can make the business relationship, the more chance you have for the relationship to be loyal and committed to you as the preferred choice. The more personal the relationship the more chance you have to gain results through that relationship.

The UNI Factor to Building Relationships

Over the past years, I've seen various reports that talk about the reason individuals stop doing business and go elsewhere for services and products. It comes down to this: 2/3 of your business and portfolio stop doing business with you for three reasons: They feel *unappreciated, neglected* or feel that they've been treated with *indifference* as to whether they are important to you and your business. I'm not kidding – over 67% of your business goes away because they think you don't care, you haven't shown appreciation or you could care less whether they continue doing business with you! That's not how you really feel about your customer relationships, right?! It's what 67% or more of your customers think about their relationship with you when they move on!

Ongoing communication and interaction with your relationships build the loyalty bond so people will never think of making a move away from you or feel like you don't care or appreciate the relationship. Part of the success in building a Million Dollar Database™ is to recognize the power of having your relationships logged and organized so you can communicate with them effectively and send personalized communication that keeps you engaged with them.

Hi-Touch Versus Hi-Tech

The power of technology allows us to be efficient with our communication, however, in our hi-tech, electronic and impersonal world, the personal touch goes so much farther in cementing powerful, long lasting business relationships. Over the last two decades business has become automated, systematic and impersonal. The key today is to use technology in such a way as to maintain top of mind awareness but in a personal, relationship-focused manner. I always tell clients that's it's an efficient thing to put your important contacts and key relationships into a system to stay connected, but never allow them to know they are part of a system.

There's also a fine balance between hi-tech and hi-touch. Think of using technology as the main ingredient to be efficient, but stamp the personal touch through your interaction and personalization of the message in communication. This allows you to be efficient in getting the job done, but personal in the manner with which you build relationships. Businesses get it so wrong when they try to automate the process to relationship building. You can't automate getting to know people! Time…patience…. execution….and a personal approach to keeping connected is the process. Use your Million Dollar Database™ as the central tool that helps you keep connected with your important business relationships.

From lunches, personal visits, cards, letters, gifts and email communication, how you stay connected is as important as who you stay connected to. Use the techniques discussed in the next chapter and you'll be working yourself into a Million Dollar Database™ of opportunity and results!

Top of Mind Awareness

Nurturing and staying connected is a way to keep top of mind when your key relationships think about using you, your services and/or products. Top of mind also leads to opportunities for connections and/or resources when the timing is right.

The more you stay connected, in front of, and in communication with those contacts that are important to you in business, the more chance you have to maintain top of mind awareness when the need comes up to be recommended and/or introduced to your services and products. People choose what's most familiar, so your job is to build a strong connection through interaction and communication. Your very organized Million Dollar Database™ allows you to do this efficiently and productively!

8

Ding! You're Now Free to Connect!

"Small Gestures Lead to Big Results"

Touch Time Counts

Now it's time to connect, to engage, to communicate and interact with your contacts and key relationships! This is the exciting part in building a Million Dollar Database™ as now you'll start to benefit and see results over time from building priceless relationships!

From previous chapters, you should have selected a database, categorized and organized your relationships and set up the intelligence gathering section in your database. Now you have the ability to connect, relate and reap the rewards from your Million Dollar Database™!

Successful business professionals know that priceless relationships are not built randomly or by accident. Building priceless relationships is more than just a philosophy, or a way of doing business. You must have a well thought out game plan like any other business strategy that makes you successful. Your goal in building your Million Dollar Database™ is to develop a plan to stay connected and in touch with your key contacts and best relationships!

How Do <u>You</u> Stay in Touch?

Before you can implement a plan to stay connected, it's important to evaluate your past activities in staying in touch with your key relationships. What have you done in the past to keep connected? What's worked best? What have been your least effective strategies?

From hundreds and hundreds of interviews with business professionals and feedback from past attendees at workshops, most professionals will admit to keeping connected through a series of letters, cards, gifts, email messages and face-to-face meetings. In addition, association and attendance at sporting events, concerts, parties, small gatherings, business events and other entertainment functions serve as key methods to staying in touch.

True Confessions

The next part of rating your efforts is to ask how <u>well</u> you keep connected with your important business relationships. If you had to give yourself a rating from 1 to 10, with 1 being worst and 10 being best, what rating would you give yourself in how well you stay in touch?

This is the part where true confessions come in. Most professionals will admit that when they rate themselves on how well they stay connected and in touch with their key relationships, they don't do as great a job as they'd like.

They want to stay in touch better, but they have challenges in keeping connected when so many other things seem to be more important and critical to success. How about you? Does this describe your situation?

What's Holding You Back

We all know that relationships are central to business success. Research shows that business professionals want to do a better job in staying connected, but challenges related to time, money, budget and resources get in the way. The bigger challenges are how do you put a system in place and make the process of staying in touch more automated and part of your overall system and game plan? What keeps you from consistently, routinely and systematically staying in touch with your key relationships? More importantly, what should you do about it?

No Time to Build Relationships

If you find that you can't (or won't) make time to build relationships and set this as part of your overall game plan, then you must be one of the few that believe relationships don't matter to you and your success in business. You've gotta' believe in order to achieve, so change your focus and know that if you dedicate your efforts to building deeper relationships with those you want more business from, referrals from and connections to, it all comes down to how well connected you are and how deep the relationship. Change your focus and change your results!

Gotta Sell More

Are you always chasing new business as opposed to giving time, effort and attention to your existing client and referral relationships? If your focus is always on the chase for new business and bringing in new customers as opposed to nurturing your existing relationships, it's time to shift efforts and put more time and attention to building existing relationships. In addition, if you're always chasing new business, shift your efforts to building referral partners and strategic alliances so you bring in the right kind of business as opposed to chasing cold opportunities.

Not Automatic

If you don't have a well thought out plan in what to do and have your procedures organized into steps one, two, three and four to execution, you're missing the boat in being as successful as you can. Organization, planning and implementation are key so you know what to do next. A few changes to your business development process can change your results.

No System

Without a master plan in knowing what stage a relationship is in development, you'll never be as successful as you could be in generating new business, repeat business and referrals. Using your database as the central tool to know what stage a contact is in can be the difference between doing good business and doing great business. You need a system to know what stage a relationship is in to convert new customers into repeat customers and potential customers into new customers.

Fear

What if you were more successful? The fear factor is one of the main challenges I see with professionals in business. Why change what you do and how you build relationships?

Just keep doing the same old thing the same old way. Have you heard the definition of insanity? Why not continue to "up your game" and be better, faster and stronger so you're more successful? Think about making a few slight changes to what you do and see how you'll reap better results! Don't let the fear factor of doing nothing and getting the same results be a hurdle. Try new strategies and be willing to execute new strategies to stay in touch.

Mix It Up

Are you always pitching when you communicate with your contacts and relationships? "Buy from me! Here's how great we are! Buy from me now!" This message gets tired and old. Mix up your communication message and use an array of methods to differentiate yourself and keep top of mind by getting your message through more effectively.

It's so boring to use the same, tired marketing message. Your relationships don't pay attention to the same message and/or method or communication. Your success in building a Million Dollar Database™ is to connect with your relationships and engage people in such a way as they want to connect back. Stop pitching and start providing opportunity to engage people through questions, interaction and providing value with a mixture of methods to build the relationship. Look for ways to engage your contacts in such a way as that they want to connect back. Communicate with the goal to uncover needs for opportunity and how you can provide assistance.

I've included a list of methods to communicate and ideas that you should use to build relationships with your key contacts. Your game plan should use a mixture of the methods noted throughout this chapter along with selecting a mix of communication messages. This becomes your game plan and part of your highly organized system to build strong partnerships and relationships. Through your database you'll track, code and implement your system so you know how often you've communicated and to who. In addition, your database is also the place to note the results of your game plan. Are you converting potential customers into paying customers? Are you generating repeat business or introductions and referrals from your communication strategies? For now, here are some ideas to mix up the methods to connecting.

Caution: All Relationships Are Not Created Equal

Each relationship category should have a different game plan in communication. Think about the method of communication with your existing customers differently than the method and message you communicate with your referral relationships and potential customers. With existing customers, your goal is to persuade them to do business with you again and refer business to you. With referral relationships, your goal is to communicate with them to send you opportunities, new business, introductions and referrals. With potential customers, you need to build trust and credibility, along with providing subtle persuasion to select you as the right choice for using your products and services.

How To Connect

How you connect with your contacts is more a matter of

choice than whether to connect or not. So many choices abound, yet most professionals seem to get set into one or two key connection methods because once you get used to something, you stick with it. If it ain't broke, don't fix it, right?! Think about evaluating how better your results could be in business if you mixed up the communication channels and used different methods to gain different results. If you're always using email as your primary communication method, what if you actually had lunch or coffee with some of your key relationships? Breaking bread with your key contacts is a great way to gather intelligence and make the social process of knowing someone central to priceless relationships.

Think of developing a master game plan where you select different methods from an array of choices and mix up what you use to stay connected with key relationships. Build out a yearly calendar of connection methods so you always know what you're going to do and when you're going to do it. In my experience, I've found that there are certain times when it makes sense to send a card versus an email message, or when it's more important to have a face-to-face meeting than using email or the telephone to connect.

Cards

From interviews and conversations with hundreds of professionals, cards are not as popular today due to the efficiency of email communication and email marketing. Cards, however, can be very effective in helping you build priceless relationships. Cards allow you to be personal in your communication. Cards allow you to stand out and set yourself apart because so many people use only email communication to stay connected. Cards can be a way to show you care because you paid attention to a life event or business event that needs to be acknowledged. Timed appropriately, cards are a great way to cement and build relationships!

The biggest challenge I hear from professionals is the difficulty of having the right selection of cards ready anytime you want to acknowledge the relationship and the situation. You need to have an assortment of cards ready at any given moment to send out when the opportunity presents itself to acknowledge the relationship. Have a selection of cards for the following occasions: birthdays, thank you, congratulations for an accomplishment or award, condolence, sympathy, get well, anniversaries, new job promotion or transition, new baby congratulations, new wedding congratulations or recognition for going the extra mile. You may even want to have cards for occasions such as empty nesting, congratulations for the kids going to college, just wanted to stay in touch cards, referral thank you cards, seasonal cards or holiday cards. There are so many occasions when a greeting card can help you stand out to show you've paid attention to the relationship!

The best way to use cards is to look for a trigger event or situation before sending a card. When a "cue" moment of opportunity happens in someone's life or business life, a card is a great way to acknowledge the event and/or situation. Birthdays are a wonderful date to send cards, however, I've found that if you pay attention and look for other occasions, (remember the intelligence gathering chapter?) the best way to set yourself apart and cement the relationship is through condolence, sympathy, congratulations, achievements or accomplishments of some nature.

Another option that I'm quite fond of is using an online greeting card system to send out your cards whenever you want. One of my favorites is called Send Out Cards, which allows you to set up an account and then send one or many cards anytime you want. In addition, you can send out cards in bulk from thousands of choices and selections. Check out www.sendoutcards.com for more information.

To build a Million Dollar Database™ is to dial in and pay attention for the right time to send cards for acknowledgement, well wishes or condolence. Cards show you care. Relationships need to be nurtured and cards are a great way to cement priceless relationships.

Phone calls
Whatever happened to the old adage reach out and touch someone via phone? Touching base via the telephone can be a great way to gather intelligence or just to say "hello" to a contact or relationship you haven't talked to in awhile.

Since so many professionals today use email as the primary method of communication, there are many times when you can nurture relationships more effectively by connecting via telephone versus sending an email. They key differentiator has to do with how long it's been since you've talked to the contact or whether all your communication is via email.

If you're looking for a method to reach out, reconnect or touch base, the telephone is a tool that's very effective. If all you use to connect with your key relationships is email and email marketing, then the telephone connection is a perfect alternative.

Use the telephone when you haven't talked to a key contact in some time or haven't had a conversation with a key customer or relationship for awhile. The telephone is a nice way to break up the communication style and connect at a more personal, relationship-oriented level. Think of using the telephone as a method to use when you want to actually speak to your contacts but the relationship might not warrant your physical time and attention through a face-to-face meeting. While not as efficient as email communication, the telephone is a great way to be more efficient than having a face-to-face meeting with a contact.

Face Time

Spending time with clients, contacts and relationships face-to-face should be considered very carefully. Like most professionals in business, you're busy and have enough things to juggle, so use face-to-face time with your relationships very discriminately. I always recommend that clients meet face-to-face with their best clients and referral sources. Face-to-face meetings should also be used as an effective tool in gathering personal information and business intelligence. If you're looking to build a stronger relationship with a key customer or contact, then a face-to-face meeting is essential.

You've only got so many "slots" to meet face-to-face each day, so you need to make the time you spend with contacts count. Start with the best of the best and note the meetings and dates in your database. I used to print out a report each month of my MVP clients and referral partners. From that list I would set out each month to schedule lunches and coffee meetings into my day so as to meet with the list of contacts that month. When the next month came around, I went to my next level of relationships and so on and so on. This plan worked well for me and my company so I could keep track of who was in the "cue" to meet with and/or connect with.

Personal Visits
Whether you stop by unannounced to personally connect with a contact depends on whether they're a consumer or business. I wouldn't recommend just popping by to meet someone at their home unless you've made previous arrangements. For business professionals, however, this can be a very effective method if you're trying to stay connected and maintain or build the relationship.

I always found if effective if you're popping in to meet with a contact that you bring something of value. In case you don't have an appointment, treats and goodies are a very effective way I used to get in to my contacts if I didn't have an appointment.

Bring something with you when you stop in or meet at someone else's office. Whether you bring goodies, treats or useful office essentials like pen pads, notepads, desk essentials, etc., bring something of value when you stop in to meet with someone. The useful gadgets or treats give you a reason to stop by unannounced. I used to know a sales professional who consistently stopped in to people's place of business, but all he brought were marketing materials of the company he worked for. He wasn't very effective in building relationships and wasn't very effective in landing repeat business and accounts because he was always coming by to "ask" for business and hand out yet more marketing materials. Use items of value as a way to bring something to the table, so you have the opportunity to discreetly say "I hope you'll consider doing business with me again" or "please consider using our services or products." This might sound a little cheesy, but it's effective.

There are some clients and referral partners who can't accept gifts or items of value of any kind. For these relationships I would suggest asking to meet on occasion at their office or place of business. When you're eye-to-eye and face-to-face with someone, you get a better chance to know the person and cement the relationship. We used to call clients and ask for a quick meeting where we would bring the coffee break or afternoon break to the office. If you have clients who can't (or won't) get out of the office with you, bring bagels or goodies to the meeting. I've rarely had this gesture refused, as once the goodies and treats are gone, the evidence is gone. The time you have in breaking bread and enjoying the treats or snacks is time well spent in conversation and interaction to build and cement the relationship.

Special Events
Another effective way to build a relationship with a key contact is to invite them to special events or functions. From golf events to sports events to concerts or business associations, there are a number of hospitality type events you can invite your trusted colleagues, business partners and clients to. These events allow you to know them in a different manner than the sales person versus client or

referral partner. Almost anyone in business knows the value golf plays in building solid business relationships, however, what if you're not a golf enthusiast or you don't like to golf much? Nothing's worse than trying to do something socially with a business partner or client that you don't enjoy or aren't that good at. If you don't like golf, don't try to force yourself to golf with clients or colleagues. Look for something else. There are lots of other things to do. The best strategy is find out what your clients and business partners love to do. Great if you can experience this with them. Also a good strategy if you can provide them with tickets or access to what they love in sports or entertainment.

Get involved with business associations or groups in your community. From trade groups to professional business associations, there's a host of groups to get involved in. As a member, think about inviting a professional colleague to your business meetings and events. One association I belong to is called Business Clubs America (www.businessclubsamerica. com). As a member, I can invite guests to our monthly breakfast events and as a member I have the opportunity to introduce my trusted colleagues and business partners to other business professionals. I've found this to be one of my most effective tools in building a relationship with other good business professionals. I make new contacts, my business partners and clients make new contacts and I feel great by introducing people to other good business people!

If you're not into sports or belong to any groups that you can invite guests to, think about hosting your own event or function. You can put together a group of three or five business professionals and invite them to lunch to introduce them to each other. I used to introduce two or three professionals at a time over lunch, breakfast or cocktails. I would pull together about two or three of my business partners to introduce to other colleagues that I thought would be possible referral sources to each other. I love connecting people that might be potential business partners. From the process, I felt great and the colleagues I connected enjoyed meeting someone new for opportunities and connections. It was a win-win. Ask yourself who you know that might be good to connect together and set up a lunch, breakfast or evening get-together. I don't think coffee shops are the most effective, as when there are more than two people, it's hard to hear with all the noise and background ambience. Keep the connection meetings to places like restaurants and choose locations suited to small business type meetings. Remember that engaged conversations that allow people to connect and relate are critical to success here.

Hosting your own special event is another way to build better relationships. Whether you call it a business open house, housewarming or special event at your office location, these events can be quite effective. An open house allows you to showcase you and your company and interact socially with your relationships without having to be in sales-mode.

One client of mine hosts an awards program each year at their office location to recognize their best clients and business partners with a number of award categories. This company provides parts to the construction industry and they like to bring together their clients for some fun each year, along with giving away awards for silly categories with their clients and business partners. It's become a tradition and any client or company who works with or provides services to this organization looks forward each year to their awards program.

At The Corporate Basket, we hosted a champagne and dessert party one year. We hosted the event in our production facility and had tall belly-bar tables peppered throughout the back parking lot. We gave away fun door prizes. Everyone had the chance to schmooze and interact. Nothing was structured, just the opportunity to enjoy fabulous dessert, champagne and the chance to meet new business people from the business community. To this day I still get rave reviews over our champagne and dessert party!

Gifts
Think about using gifts as a tool to stay connected and reward your loyal clients and business partners and show appreciation. You always recognize new customers and reward loyal client and referral relationships. Nothing's worse than sending gifts that may appear to be a bribe or incentive to conduct business with you or refer business to you.

The best way you can use gifts as a relationship builder is to look for the reason when to send a gift. In your database, you should have intelligence gathered on your best relationships. Not every client or business partner is worthy of a gift, so you've got to segment your relationships and look for the best clients and business partners as the ones who receive gifts of appreciation. I always suggest the holiday season as the last season you want to show appreciation. Everyone else is sending gifts during this time and you won't stand out or be remembered if you show appreciation during this time of year. If you're looking to stand out and be noticed when you acknowledge your best relationships, then choose another season or holiday as the time when you send gifts. New Year's gifts or Valentine gifts or Halloween or Thanksgiving gifts are great alternatives to the seasonal dilemma. Service anniversaries or client birthdays are good dates to show appreciation because you've taken the time to know when these dates are and you're taking the time to show you care by acknowledging that special day. Send gifts at the holiday season if you must and if the gesture has been a tradition. I would suggest sending gifts at a different time of year. I promise you'll be amazed at how different the response will be in feedback and kudos'.

To Logo or Not to Logo

I'm a big believer that if you're going to give gifts then you shouldn't have your company name or logo branded on the gift. Gifts with logos and business names on them of your company aren't really gifts, they're promotional items. I may strike a chord with this statement, as it's such a common thing to send gifts with logos and company names on them today. Trust me when I tell you that for nine years I observed and researched the response our clients received when they used logo items as the gifts for appreciation. Gifts that hit the mark were personalized to the individual, not branded with the company logo and name. If you must use logo items, then add other items to the appreciation gifts that don't have your logo on them. If you're sincerely looking to show appreciation to your business partners and colleagues, then make the gift personal and custom to the individual getting the gift and not as a tool to brand you and your company. Use advertising items with your logo and business name on them as a tool for promotion and not appreciation.

I used to send referrals to a local CPA firm and every time they received a referral from me I would receive a gift from them with their company name and logo on the items. While I appreciated the gesture, I never felt these items were gifts, they were a tool for the CPA firm to promote their brand and company. A better strategy would have been to receive the same items branded with my name on it. Now that would have been a gift!

Breaking Bread
Dining with your best colleagues and business partners has to be the single best method to building better relationships. The challenge is that it takes times and you have to be good at socially striking up a conversation with people. This is the best way to build referral partners and key customer relationships. Breaking bread allows you to engage in conversation, get to know your relationship on a personal level and find out more intelligence than you can ever get by meeting at their office location or over the phone. People are more social outside of the office. People let down their guard in a social setting. It's also a phenomenal way to debrief and find out what you can do differently in building a more effective partnership or relationship. I always used the breaking bread strategy as a wonderful way to look back over the past year and ask my clients and referral partners what we did well and what we needed to change and modify from their perspective to go above and beyond.

If you're building a Million Dollar Database™, then you should be sorting your relationships each month to develop a report that details who the contacts are you should invite to lunch or coffee or dinner with. I can't stress enough how valuable breaking bread with people can be to building relationships. You have the opportunity to learn so much about people through conversation. You can ask questions, get to know someone and build rapport with them like no other way.

If breaking bread isn't part of your normal follow-up strategy, try taking a key contact to lunch or inviting them to breakfast and try it out. If you do what I recommend from earlier chapters to gather intelligence, this can be a phenomenal way to glean good information to act on later and build a loyal, priceless relationship.

You've only got so many "slots" to fill for breaking bread at lunch, breakfast and dinner so you need to be strategic about this. Realize that you've got to focus on quality relationship building and not just filling a pipeline with lunch, breakfast and dinner appointments to fill the slots. Think about inviting the best clients and business partners you have that you'd like to get to know better. Each month I pull a report of both my best clients and best referral partners. I review the list each month for ones I haven't talked to in awhile or those I want to get to know better. Those relationships get the call or email for an invitation to meet that month. I also use breaking bread as an annual review and time to learn how well we hit the mark over the last year.

Breaking bread allows you to be in a relaxed setting and learn so much more about your relationships personally and professionally. Breaking bread allows you the opportunity to visit socially with your contacts and really cement the relationship for the future.

Breaking bread is also a great tool to engage and connect with a client or business partner that you have a less than perfect, or strained relationship with. You have the opportunity to meet directly outside of the office and speak socially and smooth over the issues that may have strained the relationship. Take people out of their office and get them into a social setting. This changes relationships.

I realize there are some clients that you can't break bread with. If you have clients who work for the government or companies with policies that frown on meeting others over breakfast, lunch or dinner, you will have to find other ways to get in front of them to build the relationship. Earlier, I mentioned that we used to bring the "coffee break" or "lunch break" to the offices of those colleagues and partners that weren't allowed to meet with us outside of their company locations. The key is to find a way to engage and connect with them without buying them gifts or taking them to lunch, breakfast or dinner. If the relationship is worth it and you can find a unique way to stay connected, you're on the right track!

You need to be very strategic in this manner of communication because it's time consuming and not every relationship can be dedicated the time it takes to dine over lunch, breakfast or dinner. Choose the ones you want more face time with and make notes and gather intelligence so you continue to build the relationship. Pick the relationships that you'd like to get to know better or those referral partners you're looking to build a stronger partnership with. Once isn't enough. You need to be consistent with this process and meet more than a few times over the course of a year or longer. This strategy takes time and consistency. You don't want to burn out your best relationships by inviting them to lunch each month. Once or twice a year is a good strategy, unless there's another reason to get together.

Email
We live in the digital world, so communicating and staying in touch is easy when you think of email marketing. How many e-newsletters and email marketing pieces do you currently have sitting in your "in" box right now? Not many, right?! Email communication is efficient, but it's not personal and it doesn't do a great job of building business relationships. It's a great way to communicate effectively, but it's not the best method to use in building rapport or getting to know your key relationships to build loyalty. Email communication is a great way to "ping" your contacts to stay top of mind as a reminder that you're still around. It's not the best method to build a relationship, but it is an efficient way to communicate that you're available.

Think about your email marketing and communication as a way to stay connected with contacts through education and information. You've got to have other methods to communicate or you're not going to be as successful as you can be in business. So many businesses today have dedicated more and more of their marketing budgets to email communication. Today's successful companies find the best success through a combination of using email marketing as a tool to keep connected along with other, more personal methods of communication mentioned earlier to build better relationships.

The best strategy for email marketing is to create the personal touch in communication with it. Make sure all your email messages are sent to the individual and not in bulk. Make sure the email messages you send in bulk fashion appear as though they are sent to each individual. I've said before and I'll say again that you may have your relationships set up in a system, but they should never know they are part of a system.

Handwritten Personal Notes
Never underestimate the value of a well-timed, handwritten personal note or letter to communicate and stay in touch with your relationships. There are times when cards won't do, gifts aren't appropriate and meeting face-to-face isn't the best solution.

I recommend using a personal handwritten note when you find something of value through information, articles, publicity or something of value that you heard, learned about or read about that your contact might find interesting. Not to promote you and your business, but a handwritten note that says that you learned something that the other party might find interesting. If your business partner is really into rock climbing (which you know through the intelligence you've gathered on them in the past) and you see a wonderful article on best places to climb, how perfect would it be to send the article along with a personal note that you saw the article and thought they might find it useful. This strategy can build "wow" relationships!

This is a method that requires you to be "dialed in" for information that might be of value to your relationships. It's personal and should be used in a personal manner with a handwritten note. If you see something useful that your contact might find valuable, make a copy of it or tear it out of a magazine or newspaper. Send a personal handwritten note and reference that you saw it or heard it recently and what you thought about it.

Another method I use is to regularly scan the business newspapers and the business journals to find clients and/ or colleagues I know that have been quoted or mentioned or written about in my local newspapers. If I know them, I make a copy of the article where they were mentioned or quoted, and I send it to them with a personal note that I saw it and how great it was to see them featured or quoted. If I'd *like* to get to know them, I send it along with a personal note that I thought they might want an extra copy of it and how much I look forward to getting to meet them in the future. I have found that this targeted, very personal approach to relationship building has landed me appointments very successfully with people I'd like to know better.

I also like this strategy when you've heard someone interviewed on the radio or on TV. We used to work with many executives and business leaders at The Corporate Basket, so whenever I heard someone was interviewed on radio or TV, I would send a personal note and let them know I heard them and that they sounded wonderful! (I think the exact words I used were, "You Rock!") It only took a second to send the card, but it was a way for me to showcase that I cared about our relationship and took the time to mention that I heard them. The personal handwritten note is also a wonderful way to send a congratulations note for a colleague or business partner who's won an award or accomplished something that you've learned about. Use handwritten notes to convey a personal message, private note or "just because" kind of communication. The handwritten note can go a long way in cementing a strong business relationship.

Frequency of Communication

How often should you communicate with your best clients, contacts and business relationships? It's a question that every business professional asks and one that you should evaluate regularly. If you've categorized and rated your contacts and relationships in your Million Dollar Database™ then this step should be fairly easy to implement. Think of communicating with your "A" relationships monthly, your "B" relationships every other month and your "C" relationships quarterly or semi-annually. You have to find the right combination that makes sense to you and your business, so I recommend finding a combination of monthly, bi-monthly, quarterly, semi-annual and annual communication with all your business relationships. Remember that the ratings and hierarchy of relationships change so you need to keep your database up-to-date and your contacts rated as to A's, B's or C's.

Other Reasons to Connect

Today's successful professionals use a series of communication and interaction methods to keep top of mind with their best contacts and relationships. Think of your communication plan as a way to create top of mind awareness and association by using different avenues to keep connected with your contacts. Even though your goal is to keep yourself top of mind with your relationships and contacts, use different methods to keep connected so you don't appear to directly ask for business. It's subtle, and yet, very persuasive in the long run. I've added a few more methods that have worked well to keep connected with your best business relationships.

To Announce

Create a communication to announce key updates and/or industry changes. Using industry updates and information can be a very effective method to keeping connected. Are there trends in your business that you can share with clients and referral sources? Can you alert your contacts to industry updates they should keep in mind when buying your products or using your services?

Keeping your contacts up-to-date with announcements is a great way to share good information and keep you top of mind with your relationships. Announcing new personnel or introducing new staff to your clients and referral sources is another way to communicate and announce newsworthy information.

To Educate

Can you share best practices on how clients have utilized your products or services? This is a wonderful way to describe case studies and share client results and testimonials. Another strategy is to give tips, advice or information in how to best use your products and services. Do you have a list of the 10 best ways to benefit from using your products or services? How about the most important things to keep in mind when selecting or choosing your products or services?

What educational tips can you share with your clients and referral partners that help you build credibility? Developing a list of tips and articles is a wonderful visibility booster.

To Engage

Surveys or meetings where you ask the opinion of your relationships and contacts are another fabulous way to keep connected on what people think in reference to you, your business, your service, your industry and your products and services. Get your clients and referrals partners to give you their opinion and ask for their feedback on how you can improve what you do or offer something new and different.

Communication with a goal to engage can be done via phone, in-person, through email surveys or the old fashioned paper surveys. I've found that the phone or in-person method of seeking feedback and advice is the most effective way today in getting information from key relationships. With the telephone and in-person surveys you're able to listen and hear nonverbal cues in what a person says and the manner in which they come across. In-person and phone surveys allow you to ask follow-up questions if you'd like more detail or more information. With email surveys, you lose the nonverbal cues in communication so you should only ask a few questions at a time to engage your relationships as people won't spend the time today taking big surveys via email or through the regular mail.

To Build Credibility

The real benefit to surveys and seeking feedback on opinions and preferences has to do with how you use the information.

Once you gather data and get opinions through surveys, use the information to inform and educate about what your studies show. At The Corporate Basket we used to take the pulse and opinion from our clients and ask them what gifts worked best in terms of results or what time of year and occasion hit the mark better than others. We used to get a plethora of good statistical feedback and could use that to educate our clients and tell them from our research what worked best, how and when. There are so many ways to engage your best relationships to give you feedback on what you should do to delight and "wow" them. Once you have the information, you can use this new data to educate, inform or to build credibility as the subject matter expert with the data you've uncovered.

To Be a Resource
When's the last time you asked your clients if you can be a resource to them? Do they have a need for any other professional service advisors or products? Who do you know that you can connect them to? Connecting on occasion to simply touch base and see if you can be a resource is a wonderful way to stay connected with your key relationships. The only way this method works is when you start to plant seeds that you know some great service providers and that you can be a resource to your relationships.

Start today by planting seeds with your key relationships that when they need a service provider or have a need for any kind of service or product, they should ask you to connect them with the good people you know and associate with!

To Reconnect

We all lose touch with some of our relationships. I've interviewed hundreds and hundreds of business professionals and most tell me the fear of what people might say when they haven't heard from someone in a long time is the biggest reason professionals don't reconnect. Make the call. Mail the card. Send that email to admit that you've lost touch and that you're simply reaching out to reconnect. Most professionals lose touch with relationships over time because you don't have a system to maintain and keep track of your relationships and when you've talked to them.

If you're using your Million Dollar Database™ to keep your relationships coded and tracked for follow-up, you should have less and less relationships that fall through the cracks in communication. Make a point now to focus on reconnecting with those relationships you haven't talked to in awhile and simply reach out to reconnect. Most relationships will appreciate the gesture and will thank you for the effort to reconnect.

To Gather and Collect

If you read the intelligence gathering section of this book, you know how important reaching out is to gathering intelligence. Make a strategic effort to reach out and gather little bits of intelligence over time, not all at once. Gather personal information and business information over time, and in such a manner, so as not to alert your relationships that you're gathering information. To be subtle is to be successful with this method of connecting and gathering data.

To Stay in Touch

People change jobs, they leave companies and they open and close business ventures. The more you stay in touch the more you'll learn what new developments have happened with your key contacts. Whether they've moved, been promoted or had major life events or accomplishments, staying in touch just to keep up-to-date is a wonderful method to stay aware and informed of what's happening with your relationships.

To Connect

The more business partners and referral relationships you have the more this strategy can be very effective. When you're dialed in to the needs and wants of your business partners, you can connect people to each other. Whether you set up connections one-to-one or in groups, the more you know what your key referral partners are looking for in new relationships and opportunity, the more you can bring connections together and create opportunities for others. This makes you very valuable to the people you associate with. This also becomes a way to bring the law of reciprocity into play. The more you give, the more you get.

To Appreciate

The rule of thumb in appreciation is that you should recognize new relationships and reward loyal relationships. Ask yourself if you send a thank you to those new relationships you do business with. Do you thank those who send you introductions and referrals? Better yet, what do you do to acknowledge your most loyal client and referral relationships? Loyal relationships are the accounts and contacts you should send gifts to or show appreciation to. Thank you cards are a perfect way to show appreciation for new relationships and referral sources.

To Get Personal and Build Rapport
The more personal the relationship, the more opportunity there is to build a priceless relationship. Break bread and get to know your contacts and their personal lives. Know the family information of your best contacts and relationships. Find out who they are and what they're into.

To Follow-up
Buzz up the follow-up! Almost 40% of potential business and repeat business is left on the table because professionals don't follow-up! If you've got a prospect that hasn't returned your call or responded to an email you sent, follow-up! If you've given a proposal to a potential customer you haven't heard back from, follow-up! There's a million dollars worth of opportunity to gain simply by following up!

Flag contacts in your Million Dollar Database™ with your calendar system to follow-up and keep reaching out to connect and determine opportunity. Call and leave a message. Send an email. Follow-up to ask to meet again and review where they are in their decision. Most professionals give up before they follow-up – so follow-up!

The Recency Effect

The whole reason you're looking to reach out and stay connected with your relationships is that people choose what's most familiar. The recency effect is that the more you follow-up, keep connected and maintain communication with your best relationships and contacts, the more often you'll find opportunity comes your way, either through direct business, repeat business or referrals.

There is a point where you can do too much follow-up and communication, but 99% of the professionals I know and have interviewed over the past tell me they run out of reasons and options to stay connected. Mix up the communication and you'll reap more effective results.

What's Your Game Plan?

Now that you have ideas in creating a communication plan for staying connected with your relationships, what's your plan? What's your game plan to stay in touch and maintain a strong connection with your key relationships?

9

Never Strive to Be Perfect – But Always Strive to Perfect

"The Difference Between Ordinary and Extraordinary is That Little Extra"

The Definition of Insanity

If you do the same thing you've always done, you'll get what you've always got - the same results. That's the definition of insanity. What will you do with what you know now? What's your commitment to change and reap the benefits of building a Million Dollar Database™?

Perfection – Not!

If your goal is to strive for perfection with your database in how you organize, communicate and relate to your key relationships, you're missing the boat in a big way. Never strive to be perfect as your database will never be perfect, it's a work in progress. Your Million Dollar Database™ is an ongoing evolution and always in development. One thing to realize is that your database will never be finished, it will never be completely up-to-date, and you will always need to tweak and refine how you code and keep track of your best business relationships.

Small Changes Produce Big Results

Realize that perfection is unachievable. Small steps to change and modify what you do and how you communicate with your relationships can produce incredible results to you and your business. Paralysis to action and achievement of perfection are two of the biggest enemies to business success. Start today by making a commitment to make small changes to what you do in coding, managing or communicating with your best relationships.

Choose small steps to change what you do and how you do it. Step one might be to get your contacts entered into your database or code your relationships so you can start the process of gathering effective intelligence. Another small strategy might be to begin the process of meeting and interacting with your relationships more effectively to gather personal and professional intelligence. You might benefit most by looking for key moments of opportunity to build priceless relationships by acting on the opportunities to cement solid relationships. You might find the most effective step for you is to rate your relationships so you work smarter in being effective and being more productive. Another small step is to be more connected by finding new methods to stay in touch and engage interaction with your best business relationships.

Simplify the Process

Building a Million Dollar Database™ can be complicated or simple, the choice is yours. Appendix E reviews the key points in building your Million Dollar Database™. There's a methodical process to doing better business by first evaluating who you know, and then organizing your key relationships so you code, track and communicate with your best contacts and connections.

At the end of the day, success in business is about how well you relate and work with people. It's also about how well you know your important business relationships. This may sound cliché, but people make the world go round, so the process of building a Million Dollar Database™ is how well you know people and what you do with what you know.

Go therefore and connect, relate and engage with your key contacts and relationships. I wish you the best of success in building a million dollars (or a "zillion" dollars) worth of opportunity and connections by tapping into the power through your database of who you know and how well you know them!

Appendixes

Appendix A

Ideal Client Profile

	Descriptions of Ratings	Current Customers Who Fit This Description Characteristics – Descriptions by Category (Sales Volume, Size of Company, Type, other characteristics)
		Describe by type of industry, Type of company, Size via employees or revenue, Location, Other characteristics, Person's title you interact with (Human Resources Director, CEO, CFO, homeowner, new parent, senior citizen, etc.
A's	20% of your customers who give you 80% of your results in sales and revenue These clients have a significant impact to your bottom line – if one goes away – it's a huge hit to you and your business.	
B's	These are smaller size clients but are most likely the most loyal customers you have. These clients are about 35% of your customers and are considered your "bread and butter" accounts – loyal, regular, etc.	
C's	These customers are the one hit wonders. These customers will be about 45% of your customer list and should be described as the low volume, size and one hit accounts.	
D's	These customers are your "undesirable" customers. You typically do not go after this type of business or seek to work with these type of customers in the long run.	

© 2008 Copyright Michelle Bergquist

Appendix B

Ideal Prospect Profile

	Description of Ideal Prospect	Characteristics – Descriptions (Sales Volume, Size of Company, Type of Company, Key Function, Position, other characteristics)
A's		
B's		
C's		
D's		

© 2008 Copyright Michelle Bergquist

Appendix C

Your Million Dollar Database™ System

On the next page I've outlined the system to setting up your Million Dollar Database™.

Use this handy form as a process and flowchart to set up your database and build your game plan of communication and interaction with all your contacts and relationships.

1. Enter contacts into your database and determine the places where leads and/or contacts came from and how they came to know you. Use this initial "database dump" as the first start to getting your contacts entered in the database and coded as to how they came to know you.

2. Customize your database categories as all contacts need to be entered and coded according to fields such as how met, custom profile fields, personal information, business information and relationship categories you assign to track and measure about your contacts.

3. Develop a global system to implementing your relationship coding and rating system, which includes giving a hierarchy to your contacts and giving definition to the type of contact or relationship they have to you and your business.

4. Set up your annual communication plan and assign communication, interaction and intelligence gathering to your contacts and relationships. You need to prioritize and determine how often and at what frequency you will contact your A, B and C relationships.

Appendix C - Flowchart

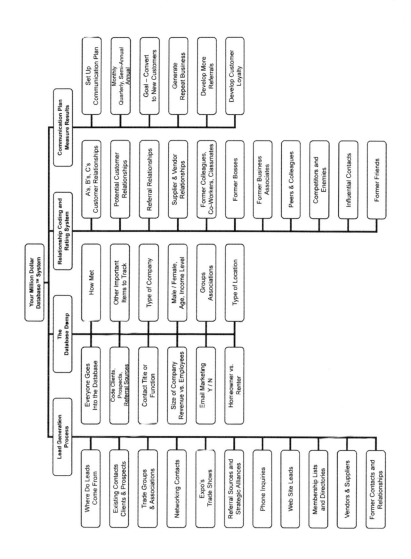

Your Million Dollar Database™ System

Lead Generation Process
- Where Do Leads Come From
- Existing Contacts Clients & Prospects
- Trade Groups & Associations
- Networking Contacts
- Expo's Trade Shows
- Referral Sources and Strategic Alliances
- Phone Inquiries
- Web Site Leads
- Membership Lists and Directories
- Vendors & Suppliers
- Former Contacts and Relationships

The Database Dump
- Everyone Goes Into the Database
- Code Clients, Prospects, Referral Sources
- Contact Title or Function
- Size of Company Revenue vs. Employees
- Email Marketing Y / N
- Homeowner vs. Renter
- How Met
- Other Important Items to Track
- Type of Company
- Male / Female, Age, Income Level
- Groups Associations
- Type of Location

Relationship Coding and Rating System
- A's, B's, C's Customer Relationships
- Potential Customer Relationships
- Referral Relationships
- Supplier & Vendor Relationships
- Former Colleagues, Co-Workers, Classmates
- Former Bosses
- Former Business Associates
- Peers & Colleagues
- Competitors and Enemies
- Influential Contacts
- Former Friends

Communication Plan Measure Results
- Set Up Communication Plan
- Monthly Quarterly, Semi-Annual Annual
- Goal – Convert to New Customers
- Generate Repeat Business
- Develop More Referrals
- Develop Customer Loyalty

© 2008 Copyright Michelle Bergquist

Intelligence Gathering Form

On the next page I've included the fields to use when gathering "intel." Obviously, some information may not apply to every contact or relationship. Use this list as a handy reference tool before you meet and/or interact with relationships. Customize the fields in your database with these sections and fields to note information as you collect details over time.

Appendix D - Intelligence Gathering Form

Vital Information
Name
Company Name
Phone
Mobile Phone
Email
Personal Email
Best time to reach

Personal Information
Nickname
How to pronounce name
Age
Birthday
Home State
College
Military Service
Health concerns – issues
Anniversary Date of becoming Client

Family Information
Current Marital Status
Spouse
Children – Names and Ages
Wedding Anniversary
Homeowner – Y/N
Business owner – Y/N

Likes / Dislikes
Sports Preferences
Alcohol Preferences
Smokes – Y/N
Favorites -
color - movie
restaurant - music
foods – snacks - beverages

Relationship Cues – Moments of Opportunity to Engage & Connect
Moving – Relocating
Family Changes
Married – Divorced
Children – New, milestones
Children / Family Accomplishments – marriage, grandkids, etc.
Family Emergencies – illness, medical condition
Family Tragedies – illness – death – accidents
Job Changes / Career Changes
Vacations – Big Trips
Business – Personal - Accomplishments and Milestones

Personality Characteristics
Talks About Most
Loves Most
Hates Most
Things that Impress
Hot Buttons
Subjects to Avoid
Conversational Interests
Gets fired up over

Business / Career Information
Position
Title
Background / History
Education
College
Significant Accomplishments
Awards
Previous Work / Career
Significant Milestones
Like Most About Career
What They're Proudest Of

Affiliations
Trade Groups
Associations
Civic Organizations
Clubs
Awards
Board Positions
Board of Directors

Special Interests
Hobbies
Sports
Recreational Activities
Vacation–Travel - Talks About
Outside Interests
Outside Activities
What do they care about most

© 2008 Copyright Michelle Bergquist

Appendix E

Steps to Building a Million Dollar Database™

Use this list as a checklist to achieve better business results as you build your Million Dollar Database™:

1. Evaluate who you know.

2. Determine who your most important relationship categories are and define them by name.

3. Select a database to house your contacts and relationships and make sure you use only one central database to keep all your contacts and relationships.

4. Enter and code your contacts and relationships and code custom fields for specific information like how you met your contacts, contact titles and other fields important to you and your business to track and measure.

5. Categorize your business relationships according to clients, prospects, referral sources, contacts of influence, former contacts, etc so you can search and sort for these categories and communicate separately with each relationship category.

6. Rate your business relationships according to good, better, best, A's, B's, & C's.

7. Develop a global strategy to collect and gather intelligence regarding personal information, business information and key preferences and habits of your best relationships.

8. Connect, stay in touch and reconnect with relationships according to a systematic plan.

9. Look for critical moments of opportunity to cement relationships by paying attention to small details and intelligence that allow you to "wow" your relationships in how you've paid attention and collected personal / business intelligence.

10. Maintain and keep your database up-to-date by jotting and noting all information into your database, along with setting a calendar for follow-up and generating reports to contact relationships according to a schedule and plan.

About the Author

Michelle Bergquist, known back in the day as the "Walking Rolodex," believes that business and success is all about relationships. As business consultant, national speaker and corporate trainer to companies and associations throughout the United States, Bergquist entertains and educates small groups, conference attendees and large corporate audiences. Bergquist speaks on a variety of business topics in relation to networking, relationship building, customer loyalty, entrepreneurship, communication skills, sales and marketing. She's most well known for engaging audiences on the power of relationships and how well you connect and relate to people determines your success in business and in life.

Bergquist currently lives in Carlsbad, California and enjoys spending as much time as possible with her family, friends, business colleagues and associates. After all, it's all about relationships!

Services Available

Michelle Bergquist is available for customized business consultation or to entertain, educate and motivate your team members, group, organization or association.

For more information contact:
Michelle Bergquist
800-438-6132
Email: info@michellebergquist.com
www.michellebergquist.com